The heart-traveller

8

Sri Chinmoy

Ganapati Press

© 2024 SRI CHINMOY CENTRE

ISBN 978-1-911319-60-3

Cover drawing: Artwork by Sri Chinmoy

FIRST EDITION WENT TO PRESS ON 21 NOVEMBER 2024

Meditation

I

QUESTIONS ON MEDITATION

Meditation

Question: What is the aim of meditation?

Sri Chinmoy: The ultimate aim of meditation is to establish our conscious union with God. We are all God's children, but right now we do not have conscious oneness with God. Even an atheist, who denies the existence of God, can use the word "God". His mouth can pronounce it, but he is not going to feel God's qualities. He is not going to feel anything for God. Again, someone may believe in God, but his belief is not a reality in his life. He just believes God exists because a saint or a Yogi or a spiritual Master has said that there is a God. But if we practise meditation, a day comes when we have established our conscious oneness with God. At that time, God gives us His infinite Peace, infinite Light and infinite Bliss, and we grow into this infinite Peace, Light and Bliss.

In the Upanishads it says that when someone is consciously one with God, he sees that from Delight he came into existence, in Delight he is growing, and at the end of his journey he will enter into Delight again:

Anandadd hy eva khalv
Imani bhutani jayante
Anandena jatani jivanti
Anandam prayantyabhisam visanti

Ananda means Delight. God is Delight. When an aspirant realises God, he realises Delight and drinks Delight. When he becomes perfect in his meditation, or when he is on the verge of liberation, he sees that the ultimate aim of meditation is to achieve Light and Delight within himself in infinite measure.

Question: What do we learn from meditation?

Sri Chinmoy: The first thing that we learn from meditation is vastness. Meditation is the only way to expand our outer existence, our limited being. Without meditation, we would never expand ourselves; but if we meditate even for one minute, we have expansion.

What does expansion mean? In our expansion, we cross beyond the finite, and the finite enters into the infinite. We have come from the infinite, but we are playing the game of the

Meditation

finite. Instead, we should play the game of the infinite in the finite body. God is deep inside us. He wants to manifest Himself and we want to be His conscious instruments. The sense of being a conscious instrument we get only in our meditation. Otherwise, we feel, "I am the doer." When the ego comes forward, we immediately feel "I can say this, I can do this; I, I, I," whereas in meditation, when we go deep within, we feel that we have become just an instrument, a channel. If a divine thought comes, we immediately express it in a divine way and become more divine. But we can only become channels when the mind is calm and quiet.

In our meditation, we always have to know what we are aspiring after. Some people, in the name of meditation, permit all the worst kinds of thoughts and desires to enter them. When distracting thoughts enter into our mind during meditation, we have to ask ourselves what we are going to gain. Nothing, nothing! The best thing in meditation is to have no thoughts, emotions or ideas. No thought, not an iota of thought, should penetrate our mind.

The mind is fertile soil. Only the divine seed should grow there, and not any outer, human thought or idea. Then, if we start meditating, and the mind is calm and quiet, say for five minutes, we will see or feel our inner being or psychic being. This being starts speaking in a different language, and through meditation we will be able to learn its language and be able to hear its message. At that time, the psychic being can mould our outer life.

This opportunity is given to everyone, but unfortunately, most of us do not try to meditate. God is inside us, but we have compelled Him to keep His eyes closed. Like a child playing, He is just trying to open His eyes, but we say, "No, no You must not open your eyes." But a day comes when we will, with our meditation and aspiration, bring the divine Child who is within us to the fore and look at Him. And we will see that the divine Child is no one other than ourselves. With our meditation, we consciously are trying to bring forward that Self of ours. Only meditation can accomplish this, nothing else.

Meditation

Question: What is the highest meditation?

Sri Chinmoy: The highest meditation is when you do not have any thoughts at all. Right now when we are meditating, we are victims to many thoughts undivine thoughts, ugly thoughts, evil thoughts. At other times we do a kind of meditation where we get fairly good thoughts, divine thoughts, fulfilling thoughts and illumining thoughts. This is a higher state. But when we are in the Highest, there will be no thoughts, either good or bad. There it is only Light.

In Light, vision and reality go together. Now you are sitting there and I am standing here. You are the reality, I am the vision. I have to look at you and see that you are the reality. Then I have to enter into you in order to know that you are the reality. But when we do the highest meditation, at that time it is not like that. Reality and vision are together. Where you are, I have to be. Where I am, you have to be, because we are one. That is why we do not need thoughts or ideas in the highest meditation. Now when a thought enters into us, we give it form. Then we come to understand what is going on, or what we are talking about. But when you see the Truth, when you see that the knower and the thing that is to be known are together, then there is no thought. This is the highest type of meditation.

Question: What is Light?

Sri Chinmoy: Light is Delight. Again, Delight is God, God the Light. In one of our Upanishads it is said that all human beings come into the world from Delight. We grow in Delight, but we do not feel the Delight because we live on the surface of life. We live in ignorance; that is why we do not see and feel the inner Delight. We came from Delight. We grow in Delight. And at the end of our journey we enter into the effulgence of Delight, we retire into Delight.

This experience we get only when we meditate. When we meditate, we get inner peace, peace of mind. Delight is visible, palpable, tangible only when we have peace of mind. Unfortunately the modern, intellectual mind, the doubting mind, the sophisticated mind, does not care for this kind of Delight, which is nothing other than Light. The mind cries for outer information or it cries to achieve some partial truth. Again, while achieving the Truth, it negates the Truth. It doubts the Truth. The mind sees the Truth for five seconds, but just when it is about to achieve the Truth, it doubts the possibility, the reality of Truth. Then who is the loser? The Truth or the mind? Undoubtedly the mind.

If we live in the heart, then the heart gives us the message of identification. If we identify ourselves with Light, immediately we become Light. Inside the heart is the soul. So, if we can live even for a minute each day in our inner existence, then we can see Light in abundant measure. We can see it and we can feel it. When we feel this Light, we feel the possibility of growing into the effulgence of Light. The moment we see Light within us, the moment we see our inner Sun, which is infinitely brighter than the physical sun, we feel that the ignorance-night of millennia is gone. So let us try to go deep within and enter into the inner Sun, the cosmic Sun, that we all have. There we shall see that this Light, the infinite Light, is waiting for us and crying for us. It only needs our conscious acceptance and cooperation.

Question: When you have a personal problem which you wish to solve through your meditation, how can you resolve it and know that the answer you get comes directly from the soul and not from the emotional vital?

Sri Chinmoy: One way to know the difference is to feel that the emotional vital has one voice and the soul has another voice. Let us take the vital as one runner and the soul as another runner. In the case of the vital runner, he runs very fast at the very beginning, with excessive excitement and enthusiasm, but he does not reach the goal. He runs about thirty metres out of a hundred and then cannot run any more. The other type of runner also runs very fast at the beginning. He is confident and once the starter fires the gun, he does not stop until he reaches his goal.

When you get a voice, immediately try to see which type of runner this voice represents. Is this the runner who will stop only when the goal is reached, or is this the runner who runs thirty metres and then loses all his energy? The soul knows its capacity and will go to the goal with utmost confidence. If it comes from the emotional vital, you will feel that the answer you get will not take you to your goal. But if it comes from the soul, you will feel confident that it will take you to the goal. If this is the case, then rest assured that it is your soul speaking.

Here is another way. When you have a voice which is offering you a solution to your problem, imagine that a vessel is being filled. If this voice gives you the feeling of a vessel being filled drop by drop, slowly and steadily with utmost inner security, then you will know that it is the soul's voice. Otherwise, you will feel that the vessel is being filled with a tumbler or a glass in a hurried manner. It will fill up quickly, but very soon it will begin to spill over the top. The other way, with utmost confidence and inner poise, the soul will fill the vessel. If you have had that kind of patient feeling, then it is the soul's voice.

A third way is to imagine a flame inside your heart. Now, there are two types of flame. One is steady; the other is flickering. The steady flame inside your heart is not disturbed by any inner wind. But the flickering flame is disturbed by fear, doubt, anxiety, worry. If you feel that your answer is a flickering flame, then it is the voice of the emotional vital. But if it is a very steady flame rising towards the highest, then you know you have heard the soul's voice. Once you know it is the soul's voice, you can rest assured that your problems will be solved, because the soul's voice has much strength, while the vital's voice has no strength.

Question: If we, your disciples, have questions about a course of action and we don't know what your will is, how can we decide what to do? Do we meditate on your picture asking that question?

Sri Chinmoy: You can meditate on my picture. During your meditation you may or may not get an answer; there is no hard and fast rule. But if you get a type of inner joy with an answer, then it is the correct answer. If there is no joy, then the answer is not coming from the picture; it is coming from your mind.

There is another important thing I wish to say. Whenever you have dreams or visions, please do not try to interpret them or ask others to interpret them, because you will be making a terrible mistake. If you have a vision or an inner experience, go deep within to discover the meaning or ask me to give you the meaning. If you have a wonderful experience, you can write to me. I may not answer you outwardly or give you any specific inner message, but I will bless you and appreciate your experience. And again, if you have a really divine experience, my inner being will immediately know.

Question: How can I purify my mind so that I can have a good meditation?

Sri Chinmoy: In your case, the best thing to do is to feel every day for a few minutes that you have no mind. Say, "I have no mind, I have no mind. What I have is the heart." Then after some time, say, "No, I don't have the heart. What I have is the soul."

When you say, "I have no mind," this does not mean that you are becoming an animal again.

Far from it. You are only saying, "I don't care for this mind, which is bringing me so much impurity and torturing me so much." When you say, "I have the heart," you feel that the heart has some purity. But when you say, "I have the soul," you are flooded with purity. Then, after some time, you have to go deeper and farther and not only say, "I have the soul," but also "I am the soul." The moment you say, "I am the soul," and you meditate on this truth, at that time your soul's infinite purity will come up and enter into the heart. Then from the heart, the infinite purity will enter into the mind. In this way you will purify your mind and your heart and you will have a wonderful meditation every day.

You have to know that the mind is almost always impure. It always brings in dark and bad thoughts. Even when it is not doing this, it is still a victim to doubt, jealousy, hypocrisy and fear. All negative things attack the mind first. You may reject them for a minute, but the next minute they will knock at your door again. This is the mind. But the heart is much, much purer. Even if you have fear or jealousy in the heart, the good qualities of the heart still come forward. Affection, love, devotion, surrender and other divine qualities are already in the heart. That is why the heart is much purer than the mind.

But again, the heart is not totally pure because the vital is around the heart. The lower vital, situated near the navel, tends to come up and touch the heart centre. It makes the heart impure by its influence and proximity. The heart is not like the mind, which is always opening its door to impure ideas. The heart is far better than the mind. But the best is the soul. In it there is no impurity. It is all purity, light, bliss and divinity.

Question: Is there anything specific I can do to have a good meditation every day?

Sri Chinmoy: Please feel that there is only one person on earth whom we can call our Dearest, and that person is God. God has to be our Dearest to the end of our lives and throughout Eternity. If we do not know what Eternity is, we can be forgiven. But we know what our life span is. So, if everyday we can renew our love of God and our faith in God, then I tell you that every day we are bound to do the best meditation.

Why do people fail to have their best meditation everyday? The main reason is that they fail to renew their love for God, their faith in God, their surrender to God. Love, devotion, surrender – this is the way. Each morning we have to first inscribe in our heart with golden letters the words "love, devotion, surrender". Every day when we start meditating we have to feel that with our whole heart we are offering ourselves to God. The day we entered the spiritual life, we offered our existence to God, it is true. But that offering was not complete and unconditional. And even today's offering is not complete. But tomorrow, or in the near or distant future, this offering is bound to be complete.

You have to offer your whole existence to the Supreme as if you are placing a flower on a shrine. You have to feel that your limbs, hands and feet are like the petals of a flower. When you feel that your whole body has become a rose or a lotus, then offer it to the Supreme. If some of you do not use the term "Supreme", then offer it to God, or to Christ or to anybody whom you call your Beloved, whom you regard as your Highest, your Supreme.

In the spiritual world it is obligatory to keep the colours blue, gold and green inside us. When we have blue, we enter into Infinity; when we have gold we enter into a higher realisation and manifestation, and when we have green, we enter into a valiant new life. Therefore, every day we try to wear these colours within. When we are wearing them we will see that our love, devotion, surrender and all other divine qualities are bound to come to the fore. And then we will become the heart's flower, the flower of inner beauty, the flower of inner divinity, the flower of transcendental reality.

This advice is bound to bring you the message of spiritual progress and inner success. Please invoke your divine qualities every day, early in the morning, and you will see that there can be no dry deserts in your inner life.

Question: I'm not as receptive as I would like to be. Why is this?

Sri Chinmoy: Our receptivity is lessened by the hostile forces that attack us. They can attack us just because our consecration to the Supreme is not yet complete. Sometimes the aspirant's mind revolts, sometimes the vital revolts and sometimes the physical or even the subtle physical revolts. If there is any such opening, the hostile forces can attack us.

There is also another reason why we are not receptive. Until we are really sure of what we actually want, the life of desire or the life of aspiration, then the hostile forces will stand between our desire and our aspiration. Aspiration brings us to the goal, to the reality, but desire immediately makes friends with our enemies. Hostile forces are always on the alert; they try to divide us. They want to separate our aspiration from our desire. Then what do they do? They bring in desire and try to kill aspiration. Very often they succeed. But a spiritually alert person will take aspiration and enter into desire in order to transform it. If desire enters into aspiration,

aspiration is ruined. If aspiration enters into desire, the desire is transformed.

In your case, if you become a victim of hostile attacks, these attacks come primarily for two reasons. The first reason is that your physical is mercilessly revolting against the heart's psychic aspiration. You can't get rid of all your undivine and negative qualities permanently because you are unconsciously cherishing negative thoughts. You still feel that these qualities are fulfilling for your outer life, your vital life. Your inner aspiration is running much faster than your physical capacity or urge. The physical is constantly playing the part of a robber. The soul is gaining something for you and the physical is robbing you and squandering it. When you receive something from the soul, you have to feed yourself with the soul's light. But that you don't do. You get the light from the soul and throw it all around. The physical gets light but does not utilise it for its own illumination.

The second reason for these attacks in your case is uncertainty. Whether you are aware of it or not, you are afraid of the Infinite that your highest part wants to enter into fully. On the one hand, you want to dive into the sea of Infinity. On the other hand, you have a feeling of uncertainty. You wonder what you are going to get from the sea of Infinity. You have to know that you are going to get the infinite wealth of the immortal Consciousness which pervades the entire universe. Your soul wants it, but your physical mind is afraid. So long as there is fear, even an iota of fear in you, the hostile forces have the power to attack you mercilessly. If there is no integral acceptance or awareness of one's own real goal, then the hostile forces are bound to torture one. But if you do not have fear and if you are sure of your goal, then the hostile forces can never attack you. If you can accept Infinity as something which is your own but which you have forgotten about, if you can see that you have always been that Infinity, then fear does not come.

Meditation

Question: How can I increase my receptivity?

Sri Chinmoy: Everyone has receptivity, but this receptivity can be enlarged. Receptivity is something elastic; it can be expanded like an elastic band through the spiritual Master's grace. The best way to increase your receptivity is to be like a child. If the mother says to the child, "This is good," the child has no time to think it is bad. No matter how advanced you are in the spiritual life, you can make the fastest progress by having a childlike attitude, a sincere and genuine childlike feeling. Then, if you want to increase your receptivity, each day before you meditate, offer your deepest gratitude to the Supreme. This is the easiest and most effective way to increase receptivity. Because you are aspiring, you have become something. Then tomorrow, if you have maintained your aspiration, you will go one step further. You never stand in the same place in the spiritual life. Either you go forward, or you go backward. If you have aspiration, then you go forward; if you have desire, if you lead the life of desire, then you go backward. So if you have lived the life of aspiration today, then naturally tomorrow you will be one step ahead. Once you are one step ahead, you have every right and every reason to offer your gratitude to the Supreme. You cannot say, "Oh, I have done it all myself." If the Supreme did not work in you, you would still be in the life of desire. But you have gone forward, and you have to feel that it is the divine Force, the Supreme, that has helped you to come forward. So you offer your gratitude to Him. Then each time you offer gratitude, you again go forward. And when you go forward, automatically your receptivity increases. Receptivity means what? It means progress. The more you receive, the more you can make progress in the inner world. Again, the more you receive, the more you have the capacity to receive.

Question: How can you stop yourself from worrying about whether you are having a good meditation or not?

Sri Chinmoy: You have to feel that there is nothing to show, and at the same time you have to feel that you cannot fool the person whom you want to show. Sometimes in the ordinary life we

Meditation

show off and feel that the person who is observing us does not actually know that we are deceiving him. But in the spiritual life, you have to feel that when you are meditating in front of your Guru there is nothing for you to show. You have only to be.

If you want to show that you are doing a wonderful meditation so that I will be very pleased, at that moment your own sincerity will go away. You should feel, "I want to be sincerity; I want to be purity; I want to be luminosity; I want to be divinity." If you mainly want to show that this is what you are, sincerity goes out of you. And the more it goes out of you, the sooner you will be exposed. Occasionally, when you are trying to show what you are, you may actually achieve those qualities, but very often false things will come forward.

As soon as I want to show something to others – for instance, that I can put the shot fourteen metres – then my worries have started. If I keep in mind that I have to throw it fourteen metres, or if I feel that I have to come in first or second or third, then my worries have started. I should instead regard the action as something I am becoming, not as something I am showing. I have thrown; that is my action. And in that action I have become whatever I have done. This is my capacity; this is my achievement; this is my reality; this is what I can do. So also, at the time of meditation, the point is not to show anything outwardly or inwardly, but to become everything. If I want purity, if I want humility, if I want sincerity, if I want divinity, then let me become these things. When I am becoming, then I am fulfilled. I will not be fulfilled in any way by showing what I am.

Question: How can I meditate with more intensity?

Sri Chinmoy: You can meditate with more intensity when you have developed real security in your aspiring life. What is real security? Real security is the knowledge that your spiritual father constantly cares for you. Just because I constantly care for you, I am trying to mould you in my own way. My own way means the divine way, the way of the Supreme. If you feel this, then automatically you will have more intensity because an overwhelming love and gratitude will flow constantly from you towards the Supreme in me. And that feeling is your meditation. Also, you have to feel that what I offer you is unconditional. Do not feel, "If I do this, then he will do something for me; if I don't do this, then he will not show me affection." You have to feel, "Even if I don't do anything for him, my Guru will still show me his infinite compassion, infinite love, infinite concern. Even if I don't meditate at all for one month, he will love me the same way." If you have that kind of feeling then you will automatically have intensity, because intensity comes when an overwhelming gratitude flows.

Question: Are there any exercises your disciples can practise to develop their will-power?

Sri Chinmoy: There are three spiritual exercises to develop will-power:

One. Hold the end of your thumb tightly in your first finger, and try to feel a pulsation only in the tip of your thumb. That pulsation is your life energy, your breath, your mission, your realisation, soul and Goal. It is all there in the tip of your thumb. Then look at your thumbnail and feel that there is your dream and reality. When an idea comes to you to do something, you will get all the will-power you need from your thumb. Incidentally, the thumb can also be used to determine whether or not a person has will-power. If a person's thumb is pointed at the end, generally that person has will-power. The more pronounced the point, the more will-power he is likely to have.

Two. Sit cross-legged in front of a very small mirror, with your back straight. Do not hold the mirror in your hand, but set it up at eye level so that you will be able to see only your face. Try to see your third eye. Inside your third eye imagine a deep hole, and try to see inward, not downward, through the hole. Go as far in as possible. When you reach your ultimate capacity try to see all your love there – the love that you have for your life. When you have seen all your love, try to imagine me in that place. Feel there is your love-field and give it to me. When you can give

Meditation

it to the Supreme in me, then you will be able to accomplish in the inner world all the things that you wanted to do.

Three. Stand about three and a half feet away from a wall. Then, make a very tiny black circle on the wall at eye level, and inside the circle make one dot. It has to be black. With your eyes half open, gaze at the circle, focusing all your attention on it. Try not to see anything else except the circle. After two or three minutes, try to feel that you are totally one with the circle, that your whole existence is inside it. Then go beyond the circle to the other side of the wall. When you go through the circle and beyond it, try to look back at your own physical reality, the reality that is standing in front of the wall. You started from the physical body but now you have sent your subtle body to the other side of the wall. From there try to look back at your physical. This will give you some satisfaction.

Complete satisfaction will come when you look at only the dot inside the circle and not the circle itself. Try to see your own self there, your own face of aspiration. Feel that you exist only there and nowhere else. Then try to feel that your existence, your face, your consciousness, everything, is replaced by me. Once you feel that your previous existence has been totally replaced by me, you will have established your inseparable oneness with me, and my will-power is bound to come into your life.

Question: How can we meditate on the soul?

Sri Chinmoy: Please feel that you are not the body, you are not the vital, you are not the mind, you are not the heart, you are only the soul. Think of the most beautiful child on earth. Imagine the most beautiful child you have ever seen. Then feel that your soul is infinitely more beautiful than this child. Those of you who have children know that parents always think that their own children are the most beautiful. There is nothing wrong in it; they are absolutely right. But think that your soul is infinitely more beautiful than your children. To some of you I have told your soul's qualities. If you know, think of the qualities that your soul wants to manifest.

Think of your soul in this way and then feel that you are the soul at this very moment. Feel that you are that – *Tat twam asi*. This is how to meditate on your soul.

Question: The spiritual life and meditation should be the simplest of things; yet I always seem to complicate it. How can I keep my meditation simple?

Sri Chinmoy: When we think that we are doing meditation, then it will always be complicated. When we think of what we are doing, whether it is meditation, physical work or even eating, we will feel some complication in the action either today or tomorrow.

True meditation is done when we are consciously aware of the Supreme. We have to know that it is He who is fulfilling Himself in and through us, that He is doing the meditation Himself. We are just the vessel and we are allowing Him to fill us with His whole Consciousness. When we are aware of this, after five or ten minutes of meditation we will enter into the very world of meditation. We do not have to do anything; we are there in that world because the

Supreme has taken charge of our meditation.

We start with our own physical and mental effort, but once we go deep within we see that it is not effort that allows us to enter into meditation. Meditation will be complicated so long as we depend on ourselves, feeling, "If I don't meditate at six o'clock, then my world will certainly collapse." But when we feel that meditation is being done by the Supreme in us with our conscious awareness and consent then meditation cannot be complicated.

At that time we will see that our meditation is free and spontaneous. God is fulfilling Himself through us and enlarging His Consciousness within us. But it has to be done with our consent; otherwise there will be no end to our complicated feelings.

For a grown-up person to surrender even to the Highest is impossible, because the mind has started functioning. But a child surrenders to anyone, even to a stranger. If the stranger says something is to be done, he will do it because he has perfect faith in the stranger. That is because he does not use the mind. In our case, we don't have faith in anybody and, at the same time, which is worse, we don't have faith in ourselves.

When you meditate, please try to feel the river or meditation flowing through you without coercion or exertion. Let the divine Consciousness flow through you. That flow is the real meditation which you have had many, many times. You can always have the real meditation if you allow the river of Consciousness to flow in and through you.

Question: How should we concentrate on your Transcendental Picture?

Sri Chinmoy: When you want to concentrate, first look at my face, the whole face. Then gradually try to concentrate on my forehead. Then try to think of the place in between the eyebrows and a little above. Feel that only that particular spot exists, and there is nothing else. Try to bring your eyes to that point and feel at the same time that you don't see anything else in the picture. Then try to dig there; go as deep as possible. Feel that you have got a knife, a divine knife, and you dig, dig, dig, and go as deep as you can. The deeper you go, the stronger will be your power of concentration.

Then, if you want to meditate, try to look at the whole picture. Try to feel that the entire picture is ready to give you whatever you want. If you want Peace, then try to look at the picture with the idea, the inner feeling, that the picture has infinite Peace. If you want Light, if you want Bliss, or anything divine, just feel that the picture has it, which is absolutely true.

To start with you have to have imagination, and then it becomes reality. Scientists discover so many things, but they have to start with imagination first. Then comes intuition and then comes realisation and reality. So, when you start, you have to imagine that this picture has what you want. Then go deep within and there you will find the reality. A day will come, in a few months or a year or two, when you won't have to take help from your imagination. At that time, your own solid inner aspiration will make you feel what the picture has, what consciousness is there.

Meditation

Question: How do you meditate?

Sri Chinmoy: Before you meditate, you should begin with concentration. In this way your meditation will be easier. Since you are a disciple of mine, you will get a picture of me in my highest Transcendental Consciousness. And then after a few months, if you stay in our Centre, I will give you a special pin to concentrate on. In our New York Centre and other Centres, all disciples without exception look at this pin and concentrate on it. When they concentrate on the pin, they feel that their whole inner attention is entering into my highest consciousness. All their attention is focused on my pin. They have just entered it and they are there, transfixed.

Then, after concentration, you will begin your meditation. This meditation I shall tell you about is only for the disciples; it is not for others. You will look at that pin and then do one of two things, whichever you feel is best. You are concentrating on this pin and you have become totally one with my consciousness. Now, as a disciple, you will try to enter into me totally, with your body, vital, mind, heart and soul. Your whole existence will enter into me, like a river entering into the sea. This is one way. Or you will make yourself totally empty and allow me to enter into you. These are the two ways. Suppose you are meditating today and you are not afraid of me. While you are looking at me, you enter into me. Tomorrow, if you are a little afraid, allow me to enter into you. Do whichever is easier for you. If you want to enter into me, you are most welcome. My heart's door is wide open. But if you are afraid of entering into me, if you feel that you will be totally lost, then feel you will keep your heart's door open and allow me to enter into you. At that time, whatever you need, I will bring to you. If you need joy, I will come into you with joy. If you need delight, I will come into you with delight. If you are not afraid of me, then enter into me. Once there you can drink Peace, Light and Bliss; you can swim in my inner ocean of Light and Delight. But if you are afraid of me, then I will come into you according to your receptivity. If you have kept your heart's door open this much, I will be in it; if you have opened it this much, I will be in it. It is up to you.

Meditation

Question: Guru, when I am back at home working, I try to imagine you as often as possible in person, but sometimes because there is so much happening, it is difficult. But often when I concentrate on my heart, I feel that it is full of light and full of joy and I was wondering if that is enough?

Sri Chinmoy: That is quite enough! Only if it is difficult to concentrate, breathe in a few times. Take very, very deep breaths and remember, remember me smiling. Remember my smiling pictures and remember how many times I smiled at people, smiled at you. If that is difficult, immediately look at the Transcendental photograph. The Transcendental everybody always carries. It is either in their wallet or on a chain. The Transcendental will do everything. You may not see the Transcendental smiling, but if you look at the Transcendental and remember one of the pictures where I am smiling, the Transcendental will be able to show you my smiling face. The Transcendental is my highest, but if you need a smile and if you concentrate on my smiling aspect, I assure you, my Transcendental will be able to show you my smiling aspect. In spite of maintaining my highest height, it will be able to show you my smiling face.

The Transcendental has everything and it is everything. If I have given something to the world that the world will forever and forever cherish, then that is my Transcendental picture. Believe it or do not believe it! You will go to Heaven God knows how many times and how many times you will come back from Heaven God knows. But if you keep an inner connection with me, then you will see that millions of miracles the Transcendental will do. Not thousands, but millions and billions of miracles the Transcendental picture will do for mankind.

This is not just a picture; it is my Transcendental consciousness. When you look at that picture, you are definitely concentrating on my Transcendental consciousness – not just on a picture or a piece of paper.

Meditation

Question: Occasionally I see a little flash of light, a tiny light that goes in your eye and travels all around. Sometimes it travels in a definite pattern and I watch it while I am meditating on your picture. What does it mean?

Sri Chinmoy: The spiritual significance I can give, and if that doesn't satisfy you, then you can go to the doctor and see if your eyesight is all right. But I wish to tell you that the light that you see is inner light, and you are seeing it with your inner vision. You are seeing a subtle light around my eyebrows or around my eyes, which belong to the physical in me. This indicates that your inner vision has accepted the physical and also is encouraging the physical. When you see the light circling around my eye, you have to know that my physical part has become one with your aspiration. I embody the aspiration of the physical in you and in all the disciples. While you are aspiring you are seeing the physical in me as well as the spiritual in me. The two cannot be separated. The light is the spiritual in me and the eyes are the physical. The spiritual is always trying to help the physical. So your aspiration, your inner cry right now is crying to be supported or encouraged or fulfilled by the spiritual.

When you think of yourself, think that inside the physical is your inner cry, your aspiration and your dedication. This aspiration and dedication will not go on in vain; they will be crowned with success. They will be garlanded by the physical and the spiritual. The physical inside you is aspiring and the reality from above, from deep within, will come and garland the aspiration of the physical.

So the light that you see is the light of the Beyond. When you see it circling around the eye, it means that the spiritual is encouraging the physical in order to elevate and transform the physical and fulfil the message of the higher reality. The physical is aspiring and a response is coming from the reality and divinity beyond the physical. Very good experience, wonderful experience!

Meditation

Question: How can we meditate well?

Sri Chinmoy: Let us try to feed the Supreme with our meditation and aspiration. For my disciples, the easiest and most effective way of doing a good meditation is to enter into me, into my consciousness. Try to remain in my consciousness twenty-four hours a day. Then only can you rest assured that you are really safe in our boat. Otherwise, you may try to leave the boat. Then I will have to jump out of the boat and enter into the sea of ignorance to rescue you. Also, to get a good meditation, one has to have inner discipline and one has to know what the truth is, what aspiration is. This requires time. If God-realisation is your sole wish, then I wish to say, please meditate well.

Question: Guru, how can we go deeper and deeper within so we can go beyond the surface mind?

Sri Chinmoy: If you want to dig a well today, first you have to find an instrument to dig with. Then you start digging and continue until you are tired. The next day you will dig again, and the day after you will do the same. In this way you will work every day and make a little progress. That is how you will one day get water. So if you want to dig deep within yourself, if you want to get Immortality-Nectar, then you also have to dig regularly in the same way. But in this case the digging implement is your aspiration. This aspiration is like a magnet. The higher your aspiration goes, the deeper inward the magnet pulls you. Aspiration is the only tool, the only instrument, with which to dig the barren soil within you. As you go deep within the earth with outer implements when you dig for water, so also with aspiration you can dig deep within yourself in order to get Nectar, which is Immortality. It is only a matter of regular daily practice.

You have accepted the spiritual life and you want to make progress. You may meditate once a day or once a week or once a month; or you may say, "No, I wish to meditate three times a day. What is wrong with me? I eat three times a day. Why can't I meditate at least three times a day? And if I spend an hour for my luncheon and an hour for my dinner, then can I not also spend at

Meditation

least two hours in meditation?" But here we have to know that meditation is not like eating earthly food. If your mind is roaming all the time, you can spend hours and hours in meditation but you will make no progress. If you spend two hours in meditation, then out of those two hours perhaps you can meditate well for only five minutes. Again, if you say, "I am selecting five minutes and as soon as I enter into meditation, I will have a most sublime meditation," usually it does not happen, especially in the case of beginners or new seekers.

So what all of you should try to do is this: if you want to meditate well for fifteen minutes, try to keep aside one hour for your meditation. Then during that hour, consider forty-five minutes as being only for your preparation or for allowing your mind to roam in the world of fantasies. Of course, this is not the ideal thing, but you have to feel that right now you are helpless. So you can keep aside forty-five minutes for your own purpose and then meditate well for fifteen minutes.

Again, you may feel that if you sit down for

fifteen minutes, you will be able to meditate well and you won't need forty-five minutes extra. You may feel that you don't have to take a few preliminary starts before you run the race. Before a sprinter runs the full distance of one hundred metres, he runs twenty or thirty metres in order to warm up, so that his body can be properly co-ordinated. So the same principle can be applied here. If it is necessary, we shall take a few practice starts. And if it is not necessary, then right away we shall cover the hundred metre distance, that is to say, we shall go deep within.

Question: I am strongly tuned to the mental plane. What can I do to enter into my inner being and feel my inner self more in my daily meditations?

Sri Chinmoy: Try to think that you have three things in your possession: the soul, the heart and the mind. In your case one possession, the mind, the intellectual mind, is suffering because it has been given very good training at Yale and now you are neglecting it. Try to take the mind as a possession, but feel that it is a very heavy burden on your shoulders. Who wants to place a heavy burden on his shoulders? Feel that you can easily take off this load; you can get rid of the gross physical mind.

Your heart is another possession. When you think of or try to feel the heart, feel that there is something inside the heart and that is why it is beautiful and meaningful. Your last possession is your soul, which represents reality and divinity. The soul needs a heart. The heart needs a soul. The soul is a seed; the heart is a tree. The seed needs the tree; and if there is no seed there cannot be a plant. The heart-plant comes from the soul-seed; then the plant grows into a tree and the tree becomes a banyan tree. But first there must be a seed.

If the mind is creating problems, feel that you don't need the earthbound mind. You have had enough use from it. Just take the heart as a plant and the soul as a seed. If you can grow into the consciousness of the seed, there will always be the possibility that the seed will germinate and you will grow into a plant and then into a tree.

Think of what will produce results. The

conscious awareness of the soul will always create something ever new and vibrant. If something constantly grows inside you which is pure, divine and immortal, then automatically things that are not immortal and aspiring in the physical mind will be transformed because of the constant growth. They will be transformed and illumined if they have not already left. If the mind still remains a heavy load, it will be transformed. All you have to do is to give all importance to the seed, the soul. Then the physical mind will leave you or it will have to surrender to the flood of light inside the heart which is the soul.

Question: What do you do when you are not one hundred per cent alert during meditation?

Sri Chinmoy: First of all, before you start meditating, breathe in deeply a few times. Very deep breathing helps conscious awareness. If you still find yourself falling asleep and starting to enjoy the bliss of sleep, at that time you should say, "No, let me enjoy the bliss of meditation." Instead of entering into other worlds you should say, "No, let me remain in this world. I won't even knock at the door of the sleep worlds. I shall stay here outside.

In meditation, movement is going on but in a very subtle, peaceful way. In it is the life that lifts us up towards the goal. But when we enter into sleep there is no life at all.

During your meditation you yourself will realise when, instead of getting a very dynamic inner thrill, you are entering into a world where there is no life at all. You should feel, "No, I want to enter into a place where there will be fulfilling and dynamic life."

Question: Is there any way to evaluate the result of our meditation?

Sri Chinmoy: Yes, there are two ways. One way is to ask the Master if the meditation has been really deep and profound. Sometimes it happens that when a seeker feels that he has had the highest meditation, it may not be true. At that time it is always advisable to ask the Master to evaluate one's meditation. If the Master is not available or if the Master is not in the physical, then the seeker has to evaluate the meditation in two ways. If the seeker feels enormous joy and compares this with the previous joy that he has felt when he has had a good meditation, and if the intensity of the joy far surpasses the previous intensity, then he has to feel that this time his meditation has gone higher.

The other way to evaluate one's meditation, which is absolutely the best way, is to see if, right after meditating, one feels totally detached from the joy itself. The seeker has to take the joy as an incident or an experience. No matter how deep or how shallow the meditation was, if he can detach himself totally from the joy or any divine quality he experienced and make his vessel, which we call receptivity, larger and deeper, then he is preparing himself for a higher and deeper experience. Whatever he has got is wonderful but he must not stay with the incident or experience that he received. If he can prepare himself for a higher journey, a higher experience, then that means he has gone one step higher through his meditation.

Meditation

Question: How can I see divine Light? Aside from concentration and meditation, what concrete or practical things can I do to see the divine Light? Also, during concentration and meditation, what kind of practical things can I do to see Light?

Sri Chinmoy: You are, using the word "practical". Here I wish to say that concentration is practical; meditation is practical. We have to know that God, who is all Light, is natural. Only what is natural can be practical plus practicable. So from now on please feel that concentration is something natural in your life. Meditation is also something natural in your life. Feel that when you do not meditate, you are doing something unnatural, abnormal, unusual, because inside you is God and the effulgence of divine Light.

You are trying either to enter into the vastness of this Light or you are trying to bring to the fore the Light that you already have. This Light that you are referring to comes when the aspirant is ready. You want to see the Light. You say you are not afraid of Light. Wonderful! But there are many people who are afraid of Light. You have relatives, friends, neighbours, who say, "Yes, we want Light." But the moment Light comes to them, they feel that they are going to be exposed. People feel that if they can hide themselves in a dark room, from inside they will be able to see the whole world, appreciate or criticise or do anything. They think that they will be in a position to see the world and pass judgement, but that nobody will be able to see them. This is their hope. So their darkness, they feel, is a kind of safety, security. When Light comes and is ready to enter into them, they feel that all their weaknesses and limitations, all their negative ideas and negative thoughts, will be exposed. But the very function of Light is to illumine, not to expose; to transform our negative and destructive thoughts into positive and affirmative thoughts.

You want to know how you can receive Light or how you can bring Light to the fore. For that you need preparation, and what is that preparation? The preparation is your pure concentration, your pure meditation. When you start your meditation or concentration, try to feel that you have come from Light and you are inside Light. This is not your imagination; this is not your mental hallucination. Far from it! When you start meditating, just feel what you are. It is a real, solid, concrete truth that you embody Light and that you are Light itself. You will see that there is a spontaneous flow of Light from within. First you will feel it inside your heart. Then you will feel it in your forehead, in the third eye; and finally you will feel it all over.

There is another way of seeing Light. While breathing, when you draw in the breath, please feel that you are breathing in something that is purifying all that has to be purified inside you and, at the same time, energising all that is unfed. In the beginning, there are quite a few things inside you that have to be purified. There are quite a few things which are hungry. So when you feel that you are feeding, energising and at the same time purifying them, then you will see that Light becomes absolutely natural.

There is another way of seeing Light. Since you have accepted our path, please look at my forehead in my transcendental picture. Then you will be able to see your Light inside me, or my Light. You will see Light and that Light you will feel inside you also, because there is only one Light, and that is God. He is operating inside me, inside you, inside everyone. But in my case I can consciously see it and make others feel it. So if you concentrate on my transcendental picture and soulfully repeat the word "Light" fifty, sixty, one hundred times, then I assure you that you are bound to see Light – either blue or white or gold or red or green – because from my transcendental consciousness I am ready to offer Light to anybody who sincerely wants it. This is the secret that I am telling you.

On Thursday at the New York Centre, when you sit in front of me, you can concentrate on my forehead when I am in deep meditation. Take your time and say the word "Light" silently, and while you are saying it, try to feel that you have formed a bridge between yourself and me. Then you will feel continually that you are entering into me and that I am entering into you. You don't have to meditate for four hours or ten hours. No. In a matter of a few minutes, if you have a soulful feeling of oneness with me, you are bound to see Light. This I will be able to do for you, and for other sincere seekers who are my students and disciples. But for others I will not be able to do this because they have not accepted me as their own.

It is not at all a difficult thing for a sincere seeker to see Light. But those who want to see Light out of curiosity may be denied by God because they only want to see, and not to grow into, Light. However, if God wants me to show them Light, in spite of their unwillingness, in spite of their disbelief in God, I can show them. But that is God's way of acting. I cannot interfere in God's operation. It is God who knows what is best for us. In your case, today you will see the Light and tomorrow you will aspire to grow into it. This is what a seeker does: today he sees the Goal, tomorrow he reaches the Goal, and the day after tomorrow he grows into the Goal. So you try; I shall help you.

Question: Why can't we get rid of all our undivine and negative forces permanently? Why can't we do it, why don't we do it?

Sri Chinmoy: You don't do it because you are unconsciously cherishing these negative thoughts. You still feel that they are fulfilling for your outer life, your vital life.

Question: Can one overcome one's fears through meditation?

Sri Chinmoy: Meditation is the only way to overcome fear. There is no other way. No matter how many injections we take from the doctors, our fear will not leave us. Why does meditation help us to overcome our fear? In meditation we identify ourselves with the Vast, with the Absolute. When we are afraid of someone or something, we are afraid because we do not feel that particular person or thing is a part of us. But when we have established conscious oneness with the Absolute, with the infinite Vast, then everything included there is part of us. And how can we be afraid of ourselves?

Meditation

The very purpose of meditation is to unite, expand, enlighten and immortalise our consciousness. When we meditate, we enter into our own Divinity. When we talk to our friends or move around, we are not consciously aware of our Divinity. But when we are meditating, we are consciously trying to be aware of our inmost Divinity. Divinity is not afraid of humanity. Far from it, because Divinity has infinite Power. Humanity, in comparison with Divinity, has no power. When we have free access to Divinity, when our entire existence, inner and outer, is surcharged with Divinity's boundless and infinite Power, how can we be afraid of humanity? It is impossible!

Through meditation, outer fear and inner fear are bound to leave us. Inner fear is infinitely more difficult to cast aside. But with the help of meditation our inner fear has to leave. Now you are afraid of fear. You have become a victim to fear because you do not know how to expand your consciousness. That is why at every moment you are at the mercy of fear. But when you take refuge in Divinity, with the help of meditation, then fear has to leave you, for fear feels that it is knocking at the wrong door. Now you are helpless, but fear will be helpless the moment it sees that through meditation you are in touch with something powerful, most powerful.

Now, if we want to conquer fear in the vital, then we should concentrate on our own inner being. But this is difficult for beginners. So I tell them that if they want to conquer fear in the vital, they should try to expand the real vital in themselves. We have two types of vital. One vital is aggressive and the other vital is dynamic. We use the aggressive vital, with its fighting quality, daily. But the dynamic vital wants to create something sooner than at once in a divine way, in an illumined way. So if we can concentrate or focus our attention on that vital, the dynamic vital, then we will expand our consciousness there. Then there can be no fear in the vital.

If we want to conquer fear in the unaspiring heart, we have to take help directly from the soul. How many of us have seen the soul or felt it? When you meditate here, directly on the

Meditation

heart centre, you have to know if you are really and truly meditating on the heart centre proper. Then, try to feel at every moment, or, let us say, every time you breathe in, that you are digging inside. This is not violent digging. No! It is only a divinely intensified feeling that you have inside your heart that you are going deep, deep, deep within. Each time you breathe in, feel that you are going deeper within. And then, a few days or a few months later, you are bound to feel a tingle; you will hear a very tiny sound. When you hear the sound, try to see if the sound is caused by something or not. Normally when we hear a sound, it is because two hands are clapped together or two objects are struck together. But this sound in the soul is not the result of anything. It is spontaneous. So, when you feel that sound inside, like a celestial gong, then you are bound to conquer fear in your aspiring heart.

Question: I am constantly bothered by thoughts during my meditation. Is there any way I can punish the mind so that it will behave?

Sri Chinmoy: If the mind becomes restless, that does not mean that we have to punish the mind all the time. What we should do is always be conscious of the mind. If the master of the house comes to learn that his long-time faithful servant has recently formed the habit of stealing, he does not immediately dismiss the servant. The servant's past sincerity and dedication are still fresh in his mind. He waits and observes unnoticed and unconcerned, feeling that his servant will turn over a new leaf. In the meantime, the servant becomes aware that his master has come to know of his conduct. He stops stealing. He goes one step further; to please his master, he works even more sincerely and more devotedly than he did before. Similarly, when we become aware of the mind's restless activities and its tricks, we have to be silent for some time and observe the mind quite unconcerned. Before long, we shall see that our mind, the thief, will feel ashamed of its conduct. We must not forget that during that time we have to think of ourselves as the soul and not as the body, for the soul alone can be the master of the mind. At the appointed hour, the mind will start to listen to the dictates of the soul.

Question: When I meditate, I sometimes feel a kind of pressure pushing in my mind.

Sri Chinmoy: In your mind, if you feel a kind of pressure, it means that your heart is invoking something which the mind feels is beyond its capacity to receive. The heart invokes, and the mind allows the reality or divinity to descend into the heart to some extent. But when it has not become totally one with the heart, the mind after a while resists the entrance of the higher Light. First try with aspiration to bring everything into the heart from Above. If there is resistance or pressure or pain in the head, all of which are caused by resistance in the mind, just think of the mind as an unruly, undivine, violent, cruel and hostile member of your family, and grab it and pull it into the heart. When you bring the mind to the heart, the divine heart, the soul will keep the mind in the prison cell of love, where there will be all protection.

It is very good from time to time to feel that the mind is inside the heart. A day will come when you will see that there is no mind at all, that it is all an illumined instrument. As the heart is the illumined instrument of God, so also you will find that what you call the mind has become a devoted instrument, an illumined instrument of the Supreme.

Question: How can we discipline the mind?

Sri Chinmoy: Try to feel that you have no mind at all, but only the soul. If you cannot feel the presence of your soul, you can easily feel the presence of your heart. Let your heart's Light flow through your entire being. When this happens, you can rest assured that you have transcended the intellectual, reasoning mind and entered into the illumined mind.

When Light grows in the heart or comes out of the soul and permeates the entire body, then the mind is automatically disciplined. If you want to discipline the mind by wishful thinking or by force, it is impossible. It is just like trying to straighten the tail of a dog for good. If you can live in the soul or even in the heart, then the Light of the inner existence either transforms the physical mind into a higher region or brings down the all-fulfilling Peace from Above into the gross physical mind. When Peace descends into the mind or the mind ascends into the higher domain of Light, the mind as you know it automatically disappears.

Question: Sometimes during my meditation I feel I am attacked by very undivine thoughts. How can I fight against them?

Sri Chinmoy: During your meditation, do not fight against evil thoughts. If you constantly fight against evil thoughts, to your wide surprise you will only strengthen them. But if you open yourself to divine thoughts, evil thoughts will find no use for you. They will be terribly jealous of your divine thoughts and will in no time leave you.

During your meditation, try to cultivate divine Love. Try to love humanity soulfully. You may say: "How can I love others when I do not know how to love myself?" I will tell you how you can love yourself. You can love yourself most successfully just by loving God unreservedly. You may ask: "How can I love God when I do not know what love is?" My immediate answer is: "Love is the transforming power in our human nature. Love transforms our life of stark bondage into the life of mightiest freedom. Love cries for life. Love fights for life. Finally, Love grows into the Life Eternal."

Meditation

Question: Always when I try to go beyond the mind, it says, "No, carry me with you. I want to go there, too."

Sri Chinmoy: That is a very good thing when the mind tells you to carry it with you. But you have to know what "you" means. At that time, "you" means your intense aspiration. You have become one with your aspiration, and inside your aspiration what looms large is your soul. When you have become one with your soul, you try to go beyond the mind. Now at that time, if the mind says, "Please carry me," you have to ascertain whether the mind is asking devotedly or with a kind of demand such as this: "I have helped you all this time and now you are going beyond me. You have to take me with you." If it is this demanding mood that wants to be carried with you into the regions of the soul, it is very bad. If it goes there, it will only create problems for you. It will say, "No, no, this place is very unpleasant. Come down, come down. We experienced much more happiness down there. Come down." But if it is the devoted mind that wants to go with you to the Transcendental Beyond, it will not create any problems for you.

It will cry for your illumination and transformation along with you.

To the demanding mind, you have to say, "No, you have created enough problems for me and now if I go into a room that is all Light, you will extinguish the Light and make it dark again. You will create problems for me no matter where I go. If I go to Heaven, you will create hell for me there."

But the devoted mind will be ready to accept the Light. True, it has created problems for you in the past. But this time the devoted mind says, "I have tortured you for a long time. I am very sorry. Forgive me. Now I want to go to the place where you are going. I want to share the Light with you. I, too, want to grow into the Light. I, too, want to become a conscious instrument of the Light."

Question: Why do you want us to meditate in the heart? I find it easier to meditate in the mind.

Sri Chinmoy: If you find it easier in the mind, then meditate in the mind. But if you do so, you will be able to meditate for perhaps five minutes, and out of that five minutes, for one minute you may meditate very powerfully. After that you will feel your whole head getting tense. First you get joy, satisfaction, but then you may feel a barren desert. For five minutes you will get something, but if you want to go on beyond that, you may feel nothing. If you meditate here, in the heart, a day will come when you will start getting satisfaction.

You have to be wise. There is a vast difference between what you can get from the mind and what you can get from the heart. The mind is limited; the heart is unlimited. When you meditate on the heart, you feel a sense of delight, a sense of oneness with something vast and infinite. In the heart there is infinite Light, Peace and Bliss. Other centres in the body have these qualities too, but the place where you can get them in abundant measure is in the heart. So you have to be wise. If you are hungry, you go to the kitchen for food, not the bedroom. Even though there may be a very small amount of food in the bedroom also, when you are really hungry you immediately go to the kitchen for food. Similarly, if you want a limited quantity of Light, Peace and Bliss, meditation in the mind can give it to you. But you can get infinitely more when you meditate in the heart. Suppose you have the opportunity to work at two places. At one place you will earn 500 dollars, and at the other place 200 dollars. Naturally you will not want to waste your time at the second place.

If you concentrate on the mind, you will not get what you want, because you have gone to the wrong place. Inner aspiration does not come from the mind. It comes directly from your heart. Aspiration is the harbinger of realisation; aspiration is the seed of realisation. Aspiration comes from the heart because the illumination of the soul is always there. True, the Light and the consciousness of the soul permeate the whole body, but there is a specific place where the soul resides most of the time. Reality is everywhere, but the actual manifestation of the Reality has to be in a particular place. It is like my situation now. I am here at the United Nations. If someone asks, "Where is Chinmoy?" you can say that I am at the United Nations, or

Meditation

you can say that I am in Conference Room 10. My presence is spiritually pervading the entire United Nations, but my living consciousness is right here in this room. If you come here, I will be able to do more for you than for others who are elsewhere in the building. Similarly, when you focus your concentration in the heart, you get much more inner satisfaction than when you meditate in the mind, because the heart is the seat of the soul. But it is difficult for some people to meditate in the heart because they are not used to doing it.

In the ordinary human life, the mind is of paramount importance. Without it we would not be able to function properly. But if you enter into the spiritual life, you will see that what the mind has mostly given you is information, and not illumination. The mind that you feed with books, the mind that you utilise to converse with people, the mind that you require in order to exist on earth cannot take you even an inch closer to God-realisation. As long as you have tremendous faith in your mind – the mind that complicates and confuses everything – you will be doomed to disappointment. Ordinary people think that complication is wisdom. But spiritual people know that complication is dangerous. God is very simple, Light is very simple. It is in our simplicity and sincerity, not in complexity, that the real Truth abides. Complexity cannot give us anything. Complexity itself is destruction. Once you are totally dissatisfied with the limited capacity of the mind, it will be possible for you to concentrate on the heart.

Real meditation is not information; it is identification. The mind tries to create oneness by grabbing and capturing you and this may easily make you revolt. But the heart creates oneness through identification. The mind tries to possess. The heart just expands and, while expanding, it embraces. With the mind you only divide yourself. The mind may try to do something and immediately the body or the vital may try to prevent it. But if the heart wants to do something, no matter how difficult, it will be done. If the mind gets no satisfaction when it tries something, it just says that there is no reality there and gives up. But when the heart does not get satisfaction, it feels that it has not done the thing properly. So it tries again, and continues trying until satisfaction dawns at last.

Let us not be satisfied with the things that we get very easily. Let us cry for something which is more difficult to get, but which is infinite and everlasting. If you get something from the mind, tomorrow doubt may come and tell you that it is not real. But once you get something from the heart you will never he able to doubt it or forget it. An experience on the psychic plane can never be erased from the heart.

Question: Sometimes during my meditation I find that my mind seems to be dwelling on worldly or unspiritual thoughts.

Sri Chinmoy: At times the mind wants to indulge in certain worldly and emotional thoughts during meditation. But the aspirant has to be very careful and not permit the mind to do so. During meditation everything is intense and if the aspirant indulges in evil thoughts, the effects become more serious and more dangerous. The aspirant grows weaker the moment the mind becomes a prey to self-indulgent thoughts.

It is the very nature of our lower mind to deceive us. But our tears and the mounting flame in our heart will always come to our rescue.

When you discover that for five or ten minutes your mind has been filled with undivine and ordinary thoughts, you have to feel that you have really missed an opportunity, that you have really lost something precious. You will then feel that you want to prevent this from happening again, and the next time you will be very careful and attentive.

Question: What kind of attitude should you have when you meditate on the heart?

Sri Chinmoy: Try to feel that you are helpless. As soon as you feel that you are helpless, somebody will come to help you. If a child is in the street, totally lost, if he begins to cry, some kind-hearted person will show him where his home is. In the inner world, your real home is your heart. Feel that you are lost in the street, and there is a storm raging outside – that means doubt, fear, anxiety, worry, insecurity are pouring down on you. But if you cry sincerely, somebody will come to rescue you. Somebody will show you how to get to your home, which is your heart. Your inner being is that somebody. This is the way to meditate. Cry inwardly. When you feel helpless, immediately your inner cry will take you to the place where you will get shelter, where you will get the things that you want – illumination, salvation, realisation.

Question: What is the best way to meditate during action?

Sri Chinmoy: During action, the best way to meditate is to remember to offer yourself, the action, and the result of the action to the Supreme. When you stop meditating and enter into the world of action, think of your action as a continuation of your meditation. When you meditate in silence, you go very high, very deep. And when you begin your daily activities, feel that this is another form of meditation which is called manifestation. Meditation in action is manifestation.

God has to occupy one's mind, and in this state of divine concentration, one should serve humanity. At that very hour, service itself becomes the greatest reward. In the field of spirituality, although meditation and concentration constitute a totally different approach, work and dedicated service are nothing short of pure meditation.

In all your activities try to feel the presence of God. While you are feeding your child, feel that you are not feeding your child but rather the God within him. While you are talking to someone, feel that you are talking to the Divinity within him. You need not go to your shrine and meditate on God with tears of devotion if at that very moment you have something most important to do in the outer world. Whatever you do, please try to think that you are given the opportunity to do that by God; think that you are doing something which is ultimately leading you towards your realisation.

Meditation

Question: How do you go about emptying your mind in order to be able to meditate?

Sri Chinmoy: First, you have to aspire. Then, you have to make your mind vacant. You should not allow any thought to enter into your mind and take shape. Suppose a name comes. As soon as the first letter of the name appears, you kill the name. You have to make your mind vacant, as empty as possible.

Question: How do you do it?

Sri Chinmoy: With your power of concentration. Suppose a thought, or a vibration, or something else is coming. Immediately, shoot an arrow and pierce it into pieces. An idea comes, somebody's name comes, or some thought comes. Immediately, just throw it out. It must not come and enter into your mind. Before it touches your mind you have to cut it into pieces. But if you already have thoughts and ideas within you, within your body, within your mind, then you have to meditate like this: be as relaxed as possible. Feel as if you were inside the ocean. Then absorb those thoughts and ideas so they do not have a separate existence. They are lost in the sea. If they are already within you, throw them into the sea. If they are coming from outside, then do not allow them to enter into you. After doing this your meditation is bound to be successful.

Question: How should we meditate on the picture of a spiritual Master?

Sri Chinmoy: When we meditate in front of the picture of a spiritual Master, we should try always to identify ourselves with the consciousness of the spiritual Master which is embodied in the particular picture. If we want to identify ourselves with his consciousness, then the first thing we have to do is to concentrate on the whole picture. Gradually, we should bring our focus of attention to only the face, then to between the eyebrows and a little above, which is where his actual inner, spiritual wealth can be found. This is the third eye, the place of vision, and the moment we can identify ourselves with the vision of inner reality, we shall achieve the greatest success.

If you want to get purity as you look at the picture, imagine that you are breathing in simultaneously with the Master for five minutes before you start your meditation. You should feel that he is also breathing – the Master and disciple must breathe in together for five minutes.

Question: When I meditate, I imagine you giving me a blessing at that moment. Is this blessing real?

Sri Chinmoy: Yes. When you meditate and you feel that I am blessing you, this blessing is absolutely real. But it is not my physical being that is blessing you, it is my inner being, which is totally one with me. It is like a storehouse in which I know where everything is kept. I bless my disciples with the help of my inner beings. When you see that I am blessing you, this experience is absolutely real. My physical mind may not know that this is taking place, but my inner being will definitely know. The most important thing is for my inner being to know what is happening in your life. My physical being sees only what is around me, but the subtle beings inside my physical are now in New York, in Canada, and in many other places. They are roaming and bringing me news which is all being recorded. But if there is something very important, absolutely urgent, these subtle beings will bring the news to me even while I am talking. They will ask me to stop talking and they will let me know what has happened.

Question: Was the Peace and inner Bliss that I felt here last Wednesday night a sign that I had been initiated?

Sri Chinmoy: Last Wednesday I did not intend to actually initiate anybody, but when you stood in front of me, your soul immediately recognised my status and, like a child of two years, your soul threw itself into my lap and received all the blessings – Bliss, Peace, Love and Power – from the Supreme. I emptied the inner cup that was full of ignorance and impurity and replaced them with Peace, Bliss and Purity. Although this was not a formal initiation, I can say that you were initiated that night.

Meditation

Question: How do you learn to concentrate?

Sri Chinmoy: One cannot meditate well unless one knows how to concentrate. At first the seeker should not meditate but only try to concentrate. Then after two weeks, a month, or if necessary two months, he can start meditation.

What do we mean by concentration? We mean inner vigilance, alertness. There are thieves all around us and within us. Who are the thieves? Fear, doubt, worry and anxiety. These inner thieves are the real thieves, not the thieves who steal our money. When we start to concentrate, we have to feel that we will not allow any thieves to enter into our minds. When we are concentrating, we make it hard for hostile forces to enter into us. Otherwise, we become victims to the undivine effects of the wrong forces.

Please try this exercise to develop concentration. In Sanskrit it is called *tratak*, which means "gazing". First wash your eyes properly with cold water, not warm water or hot water. Then make a very small circle on the wall at your own eye-level, and inside it make a dot. It should be black, not blue or red or any other colour. Then stand facing a wall. There should be a distance of about three and a half feet between you and the wall. Focus your attention on the circle with your eyes relaxed and half open. The force of your concentration should come from the middle of your forehead. After three or four minutes, open your eyes fully, and then try to feel that your eyes have covered your whole body. Feel that from head to foot you are all eyes. Your whole physical existence has become nothing but vision. Then please concentrate on the dot inside the circle. Then you have to start making the object of your concentration smaller. After a few seconds try to feel that your whole body has become as tiny as this dot on the wall. Try to feel that the dot is another part of your own existence. Then you will enter into the dot, pierce through it and go to the other side of the dot. From the other side, you have to look back and see your own body. Your physical body is on one side, but on the strength of your concentration you have sent your subtle body through the point of concentration into the object. Your subtle body is now on the other side. Through your subtle body you see your physical body and through your physical body you see your subtle body.

When you began to concentrate, the existence in your physical body became all vision. At that time the dot was your reality. When you entered into the dot, then vision and reality become totally one. You are the vision and you yourself are the reality. When you look back at yourself from the dot, the process becomes reversed. Now you are the vision there, and the place to which you are returning is your reality. At this time, again the vision and the reality become one. When you can see it in this way, your concentration is absolutely perfect.

If you can concentrate and go to the other side of the point you were calling reality, your whole existence will be far beyond the vision and the reality. The moment you can feel that you have transcended your vision and your reality, you have boundless power. You will be able to use this power of concentration for your spiritual life, for your intellectual life, while working, while cooking, while doing anything.

Question: The moment I sit down to meditate, all kinds of silly or ugly thoughts come into my mind. Is there any specific technique you can recommend to help me overcome these thoughts?

Sri Chinmoy: First you have to determine whether the thoughts that are attacking you are coming from the outer world or from deep within. In the beginning, it is difficult, I must say, to distinguish the thoughts that are coming from outside from those that are arising from inside you. But gradually you will be able to feel that some thoughts are coming from outside, and these thoughts can be driven back faster than the thoughts that attack you from within. So it is better that each of you right now fight with the outer thoughts first and deal with the inner thoughts later on.

When you see that a thought is about to enter you, please try to muster your soul's will from your heart and bring it right in front of your forehead. The moment your soul's will is seen by the intruding thought, the thought is bound to disappear.

Now I wish to speak about thoughts that you have already accumulated within you. When you see a thought arising from deep within you and when that thought is not divine, but absolutely impure and unlit, then immediately you should try to do one of two things. Try to feel that there is a hole right at the top of your head and then make that thought flow out like a river which goes only in one direction and does not come back. It is then gone and you are freed from it. The other method is to feel that you are a boundless ocean, with its calm, quiet feeling of tranquillity, and that the play of the fish is on the surface. The ocean pays no attention to the ripples of the fish.

Question: It is difficult for me to concentrate on my heart for longer than just a few minutes. Is there any advice you can give me?

Sri Chinmoy: When you concentrate on the heart, the first thing you should try to remember is love. Love means the victory over time. You have all love, all affection, all concern for your husband and son. When they fall sick or need you, you will spend hours and hours with them. You are at their disposal twenty-four hours a day; you are ready to give them everything because of your love. Now, your dear ones are with you for fifty years or sixty years and then they leave you. But you have to know that inside your heart is someone who is infinitely dearer than your husband and children, and that is God. In this world you have some dear ones for a few years, and then you give them everything you can. It seems there is no end to the love you offer them. But the dearest One you will have for all Eternity, and if you want to offer Him your love, naturally it will be all infinite and eternal.

If you concentrate on your heart and soulfully repeat a few times, "Love, love, love," then you will see that love is extending its own horizon. It is identifying itself with time and, again, it is going beyond time, because it needs fulfilment. When love wants fulfilment, it will not stay with time for five or ten minutes. It will extend throughout Eternity. If you know this and meditate on your heart, then the expansion of time comes, the expansion of delight comes, the fulfilment of the soul comes. If you try to feel love, you will extend the capacity of your aspiration, extend the capacity of your realisation and extend the capacity of your oneness with the entire world.

Question: When we want to concentrate or meditate on a special thought or problem, how should we do it?

Sri Chinmoy: First let us consider a problem. You have to know the seriousness of the problem. If it is a serious problem, naturally you will have to meditate on it for a long time. If it is not serious, you can solve the problem in a few minutes. If you concentrate on any problem, big or small, think of it as something made of glass. If you drop glass, it will break. It is brittle and fragile, and at any moment it will give way. If you think of a problem in this way, you will find that this is the easiest way to solve it. But if you take it as something very heavy or solid, you will not be able to solve it.

Now let us take a thought. You will say that

naturally you concentrate only on good thoughts. But unfortunately, we do unconsciously meditate on bad thoughts. Jealousy, doubt, suspicion – all these we cherish unconsciously. When this kind of bad thought comes, you have to feel that the bad thought represents a person. Just think of jealousy, fear, doubt and hypocrisy as people, and immediately give them a human form: "This fellow has undivine qualities." When it is a good thought, also give it form: "This man has all good qualities – humility, sincerity and so on."

Then what do you do? When you see a good man, feel that he is leading you and try to follow him as long as he wants you to. But if you see a bad man – a man full of fear, anxiety and so forth – feel that he is going to chase you mercilessly and that you have to immediately run away from him. You must never allow him to come near you. When you see someone destructive in front of you, immediately react as though he will destroy you. Feel that your very life is in danger. Very often in the spiritual life, people do not take bad thoughts seriously enough. We cherish these undivine qualities and feel that they are only insects pinching us. But when you have these undivine qualities, you have to feel that they are worse than dragons, something very dangerous.

Question: In our meditation, can we consciously invoke our soul? And if so, how?

Sri Chinmoy: In your meditation you can consciously invoke your soul and bring its presence to the fore. In fact, that is one of the fastest ways to realise God. But it all depends on how much benefit you want to get from the soul's presence. I am in front of you right now. You know that a God-realised man is in front of you. You are seeing me, and many other people are seeing me. If somebody has more aspiration than you, then naturally that person will get more benefit, more achievement, more fulfilment from my presence than you will. When you bring the soul to the fore, you make very fast progress if your aspiration is intense.

Now, if you know that when the soul comes forward you make faster progress, how can you bring the soul to the fore? This is the easiest way: when you start meditating, feel that you do not have the body, you do not have the vital, you do not have the mind, you do not have even the heart – you have only the soul. The only thing in your possession, the soul, is the most precious thing on earth.

Next, feel that the thing that you cherish most, treasure most, should become your whole life. Do not feel that you have to possess it; feel that you have to grow into it. When you are in a very deep meditative mood, all of you cherish me, your Guru. Why? Because you feel that your Guru has realised something, has achieved something. This is your first realisation. Your second realisation should be that it is not enough just to feel that I have realised something; you also have to grow into that realisation.

If you cry for the soul to come forward, and feel that you have to grow into the divinity of the soul, the soul will feel that you need it, and see that you want to become it. When your earthly desires have faded away, and only the heavenly aspirations remain in your life, at that time the soul is bound to come to the fore because it feels that you are ready to receive it.

Question: Would you speak a little about proper breathing in meditation?

Sri Chinmoy: If you are a beginner and want to breathe correctly, you should sit with your spinal cord erect. Now, while breathing, you have to think first of purity. Another thing can be done to further develop this sense of purity in the breath. For a few minutes, try to imagine a flower or a candle flame or incense – something that represents purity – right in front of your nose. This will automatically give you a sense of purity and convince the physical mind. When you breathe in, if you feel consciously or unconsciously that the breath is coming directly from God, from Purity itself, then the breath can be purified.

When you breathe in, try to breathe in as slowly and quietly as possible, so that if somebody placed a tiny thread in front of your nose, it would not move at all. And when you breathe out, try to breathe out even more slowly than when you breathed in. If possible, leave a short pause between the end of your exhalation and the beginning of your inhalation. If you can, hold your breath for a few seconds. But if it is difficult, do not do it. Never do anything that will harm your organs or respiratory system.

Each time you breathe in, try to feel that you are bringing into your body Peace, infinite Peace. Now what is the opposite of Peace? Restlessness. When you breathe out, please try to feel that you are expelling the restlessness of your inner and outer body, and the restlessness that you see all around you. When you breathe this way, you will find restlessness leaving you. After practising this a few times, please try to feel that you are breathing in Strength and Power from the universe, the cosmos. And when you exhale, try to expel your fear. When you breathe out, all your fear will come out of your body. After doing this a few times, try to feel that what you are breathing in is Joy, infinite Joy, and what you are breathing out is sorrow, suffering and melancholy.

Another thing you can try when you breathe in is to feel that you are breathing in not air, but cosmic energy. Feel that tremendous cosmic energy is entering into you with each breath, and that you are going to use it to purify yourself: your body, vital, mind and heart. Feel that there is not a single place in your body that has not been occupied by the flow of cosmic energy. It is flowing like a river inside you. When you feel that your whole being has been washed or purified by the cosmic energy, then feel that you are breathing out all the rubbish inside you, all the undivine thoughts, impure actions, obscure ideas. Anything inside your system that you call undivine, anything that you do not want to claim as your own, feel that you are exhaling it.

This is not the traditional yogic Pranayama, which is more complicated and systematised. But what I have just told you is the most effective spiritual method of breathing. If you practise this method of breathing, you will soon see that what you are doing is not imagination; it is reality. In the beginning you have to use your imagination, but after a while you will see and feel that it is not imagination at all, but reality. You are consciously breathing in the energy which is flowing all around you in the cosmos, purifying yourself, and emptying yourself of everything undivine. But this breathing has to be done in a very conscious way, not in a mechanical way. If you can breathe this way for five minutes every day, you will be able to make very fast progress.

When you reach a more advanced stage, when you breathe do not feel that your breath is coming and going only through your nose. Feel that you are breathing in through your heart, through your eyes, through your nose, through your pores. Now you are limited to breathing only through the nose or the mouth, but a time will come when you will know that any part of the body can breathe. Spiritual Masters can breathe even with their nose and mouth closed. When you have perfected this spiritual breathing, you will feel that all your impurity and ignorance is gone. What has come to replace your ignorance and your imperfection is God's Light, God's Peace and God's Power.

Meditation

Question: How can we know whether we are meditating well or not?

Sri Chinmoy: We can easily know whether we are meditating well or not just by the way we feel and see and think. Right after our meditation, if we have a good feeling for the world, then we know our meditation was good. If we see the world in a loving way in spite of its imperfections, if we can love the world even while seeing its teeming imperfections, then we know that our meditation was good. And if we have a dynamic feeling right after meditation, if we feel that we came into the world to do something, to become something, this indicates that we have done a good meditation. This feeling that we have to do something does not mean that we are feeding our human ambition. No! The moment we try to feed our ambition, it will entangle us like a serpent. What we have come into the world to do is what God wants us to do. What we have come into the world to become is what God wants us to become. What God wants us to do is to grow into His very image. What God wants us to become is His dedicated instrument. During our meditation if we get the feeling that God wants us to grow into His very image, wants us to be His dedicated instrument, and if this feeling is translated into action after our meditation, then we can be sure that we were meditating well.

But the easiest way to know if we have had a good meditation is to feel whether Peace, Light, Love and Delight are coming to the fore from within. Each time Light comes forward, or Love comes forward, or Peace or Delight comes forward, the whole body will be surcharged with that divine quality. When we have this experience we know that we have done a very good meditation. Each time divine qualities come to the fore, we are bound to feel that we are remembering a forgotten story. It is only through meditation that we can remember our forgotten story. This story was written by the seeker himself, by the seeker in us. The story was not written by somebody else. It is our own creation, but we have forgotten it, and it is meditation that brings it back. When we remember this story we are overjoyed that we have created such a beautiful story and that this is our life story.

Meditation

Question: Is there anything I can do to always have a good meditation?

Sri Chinmoy: It is your wish to have always most delicious food. But sometimes the food is not so good. If you want to get always very delicious food, you need to have access to an expert cook. I am your spiritual cook and you can easily have access to this cook. How? Through gratitude, the gratitude that is inside the heart, not inside the mind.

I always say that the past is dust. But sometimes, just for a fleeting second, you can remember that once upon a time you were on the same footing as your friends and neighbours. Now look at the difference between you. It is like day and night. They may be rich on the material plane, but on the spiritual plane they are poverty-stricken, bankrupt. So when you see the difference, automatically a spring of gratitude will well up inside you. If you can have a drop of gratitude, inside that gratitude you will find a new creation. A tiny grain of gratitude means a world of new creation. The seed has to be sown; then it starts germinating and grows into a plant. So, when you are not getting a good meditation, the best thing is to think of what you were and what you are going to become. Once upon a time you could not even crawl; now you are running in the spiritual life. See the difference, and then you are bound to have gratitude. To whom? To the Supreme, for He is the Doer. It is He who has inspired you and acted in and through you. He has inspired you and He has given you the fruit of your action, so naturally your gratitude comes to the fore.

Question: When I meditate with my heart on your picture I've been getting a headache.

Sri Chinmoy: You are pulling beyond your capacity. You feel you are meditating inside your heart, but you are being misguided. Actually you are meditating in your mind, but you are not able to feel the presence of your mind. If you really meditate on your heart you will develop the sense of identification. Then no matter how intensely you meditate, there can be no such problem.

Please be more conscious; then you will be

able to discover that you are meditating in the mind. If you meditate in the heart, then no matter how many hours you meditate or how much Peace, Light and Bliss enters into your heart, you will not get headaches.

Question: How can one discipline the mind during meditation?

Sri Chinmoy: It is only during meditation that you get the opportunity to discipline the mind. When you are not in meditation you will see that each thought or idea is composed of words. If you enter into an idea you will see that it is formulated with words. Words come and form a sentence either inside or outside your mind and there you get an idea. But during deep meditation, you do not need words to form an idea. There the idea comes in a flash in the form of light, or light will bring the idea right in front of your vision. At that time you will immediately see the incident or truth that you want to envision in your life.

How can you discipline your mind during meditation? You can discipline the mind only by forgetting the existence of the mind and feeling that you do not have a mind. You may think, "If I do not have a mind, then how can I exist? I will become an idiot without a mind." But I tell each and every one of my disciples that the mind you get from books, the mind you utilise while conversing with people, the mind you require in order to exist on earth, cannot take you even an inch towards God-realisation. It is lame. It is blind. It is deaf. The mind is your enemy.

During meditation if you can really make yourself feel that you have only the heart, or if you can feel that you do not even have the heart, but that your whole existence from the sole of your foot to the crown of your head is the soul, then you will see that the mind does not exist. But if you cannot feel the presence of your soul, you can easily feel your heart's presence and your heart's glow. When you see light glowing in the heart or in the soul, you can rest assured that you have already transcended the intellectual mind. At this stage you have entered into the illumined mind, which is very different from the reasoning, intellectual mind.

When the light grows in the heart or the light

comes out of the soul and permeates the entire body, at that time the mind is automatically disciplined. If you want to discipline the mind by hope, it is impossible. It is just like straightening the tail of a dog. But if you can live in the soul or even in the heart, then the light of the inner existence either transforms the physical mind and brings it into the higher regions, or it brings down the all-fulfilling peace from above into the gross physical mind. When peace descends or the mind ascends into the higher domain of light, at that time the mind automatically disappears.

Question: After I have a good meditation I lose it. What can I do to maintain my meditation?

Sri Chinmoy: Consciously, you don't want to preserve the treasure. Either you mix with unaspiring people or you don't want to preserve your meditation. You are not valuing the treasure. You think: "Even if I lose it I will get it again tomorrow." No, you have to value it, preserve it in the heart-pocket. I always tell you to assimilate your meditation. Once you eat something you must assimilate it.

Question: What should we imagine if we are very tired during our morning meditation?

Sri Chinmoy: Just imagine a blue-green forest or field. Feel that you are walking through a paddy field. Then, no matter how much you are suffering from lack of sleep, you will feel energised.

Question: How can one still one's mind in meditation?

Sri Chinmoy: Try to breathe in as slowly and as quietly as possible, so that if you place a tiny thread right in front of your nose it will not even move. Then you will see that your meditation is going to be deep and your mind will be very calm and quiet.

Then, imagine something very vast, and calm and quiet. When you start meditating, feel that inside you is a vast ocean and that you have dived deep within. There at the bottom it is all tranquillity, tranquillity's flood.

The most important thing is practice. Today your mind acts like a monkey. This restless mind is knocking all the time at your heart's door and disturbing the poise of the heart. In this world everybody has pride, vanity and self-esteem. So if you keep your heart's door closed each time the mind comes, if you do not pay any attention to the mind, then after some time the mind will find it beneath its dignity to bother you. I have seen where my disciples did not open their heart's door when the mind started knocking. They did not give a response from the heart, and the heart remained unperturbed. The heart opened its door wide only to the soul's Light, and listened only to the dictates of the soul.

Thought is from the mental world. But you also have the heart, the identification-world. When you remain in the heart, that means that you are identifying yourself with the soul. The soul is beyond ideas, beyond thought. Instead of concentrating on the mind proper, if you can focus all your concentration on the heart, then the reality that looms large inside the heart automatically gives you an access to the soul. If you concentrate and meditate on the reality that is inside the heart, this reality comes forward.

If you concentrate in the mind, naturally thought will come and bother you. But if you concentrate on the heart, then the problem is solved. So always try to meditate on the heart and try to bring the soul to the fore. The soul, which is a direct representative of God, is the eternal reality in us.

Question: How can I recognise a spiritual experience as such?

Sri Chinmoy: In your case it is easy. Millions of times you have had the feeling of true eagerness to help humanity, and with God's Grace you have helped humanity according to your capacity. Then you have gotten joy. But do not take this joy as the result of your action. When you have inner joy, please do not feel that it is the result of a fulfilled desire or a successful action.

Do not feel that you are happy because the result is satisfactory. No, immediately separate yourself from your action. Then you will see that the joy you are having is from a feeling of oneness – oneness with the universal Consciousness or cosmic Consciousness or your own consciousness.

Spirituality is always natural. Anything that is unnatural can never be spiritual. Right now, you are not seeing truth as your birthright. Truth is something unnatural; somebody else possesses the truth, but you do not possess it. But when you are in the spiritual life, you see that spirituality is everybody's property.

In your case, spiritual experiences you have had many, many times. Whenever I concentrate on you, I do see that you want to be illumined and guided by the Supreme. This very idea that you want to be illumined, guided or moulded by somebody who knows how to guide and mould you, is not a desire. It is more than an aspiration even. What it is, is an outer expression of your soul's inner experience. It is your soul that is having this inner experience. An unaspiring person says, "I have to save myself. I have to do everything. Nobody will do anything for me." But in your case, I have seen many times that you have the desire to be helped and guided by the Supreme in me. This is the highest, or you can say, the most effective experience of your soul, expressed in the form of desire or in the form of aspiration. So constantly you are getting experiences when you feel that you are a child in the Lap of the Supreme. That very feeling, you will see if you go deep within, is an experience which is embodied by your soul, and only you are trying to manifest it in the form of aspiration.

Question: I would like to know the best and the most effective way to raise one's consciousness and to maintain that level.

Sri Chinmoy: The best way to raise your consciousness is through inner cry. Then, in order to maintain your consciousness there on the highest level, you have to establish considerable purity in the vital. First, with your inner cry, your aspiration, you go up; then, through purity in the vital you will be able to stay there for good.

Question: Does sexual indulgence prevent one from acquiring occult power through Kundalini Yoga?

Sri Chinmoy: Kundalini Yoga is the Yoga of absolute purity. It is one of the most sacred Yogas and physical, vital, mental and psychic purity is of paramount importance. The three major nerves – *ida, pingala and sushumna* – will suffer immensely and immediately if there is any sexual indulgence. And it is not only physical relations that are bad. If somebody enjoys lower vital thoughts, impure thoughts, in the mind, that is also harmful. There are many who have concentrated on the centres and who were about to open them when unfortunately they entered into the lower vital world.

There are many Indian spiritual seekers who have said that when the kundalini is awakened, the vital heat, dynamic heat inside the subtle body very often causes them great discomfort. This energy comes from the subtle body, but it is felt in the physical body. Very often seekers who are about to develop spiritual powers find that the intense inner power is too difficult to bear. So they enter into the ordinary lower vital world and lose the kundalini experience.

To have the kundalini experience for a minute or two or for a few days is not difficult. The most difficult thing is to open up the centres. But this is not the end of our journey. Opening up the centres will give us psychic power or occult power or spiritual power. But the most important thing is to live in the Divine Consciousness.

If one really wants to learn occultism, two things have to be totally shunned. I am talking of strict occultism, not black magic and all that, which anyone can practise. The two things to be shunned are fear and sex. If there is any fear, either in the physical or in the mental or in the psychic, then the great dynamic occult powers can never be developed. And if there are lower vital movements, sex indulgence and impure thoughts in the being, then no occult power can enter.

Question: Is there a particular centre I can meditate on in order to control my thoughts?

Sri Chinmoy: Now if you want to control your thoughts, you should concentrate on the centre between the eyebrows. If you become very stiff and your concentration is intense, then you should not concentrate here for more than two minutes. Otherwise, you will become exhausted in the beginning.

Now, if you concentrate on the heart centre, you will get peace, love and joy. Try to hear the cosmic sound, the soundless sound, when you enter into the heart. If you bring love, joy, peace and bliss up from the heart to the centre between the eyebrows, then you will see that there will be no thoughts.

The heart is the safest place for you to concentrate and meditate on. If you do this, automatically you will get purification, because inside the heart is the soul and the soul is one with the Infinite. It is from here that you will get everything.

Question: What is the relationship between the third eye and the heart centre?

Sri Chinmoy: Let us say that the heart is Consciousness and the third eye is Light, although there is no actual difference between the two. The third eye or ajna chakra can annul or destroy the previous karma, it can expedite the present evolution and it can bring to the fore the future wealth. The third eye has infinite Light and at the same time is infinite Light; and the heart or anahata chakra possesses infinite Consciousness and at the same time is infinite Consciousness. These two are eternal friends. This moment the infinite Light – which I am calling the third eye – is a building; and inside it is the heart, which is the resident. But the moment the infinite Consciousness – which I am calling the heart – can become the building, the third eye will become the resident. Like this they constantly change.

Although Consciousness and Light are inseparable, some spiritual Masters have seen Light before Consciousness and others have seen Consciousness before Light. The one which they see first, they feel is the Source of the other. It is like this. These two fingers are on the same hand. Suppose the name of this finger is Light and the name of this finger is Consciousness. If you see the one called Light first, then immediately you will say, "The Source is Light." And you will see that Consciousness itself is inside this Light. But if you see the Consciousness-finger first, then you will say, "The Source is Consciousness." And you will see that Light is inside this Consciousness. Some spiritual Masters of the highest order see Consciousness first, while others see Light first. And depending on which they see first, they feel that the Source of everything is either Light or Consciousness.

But a time comes when they see that both Light and Consciousness are inseparable. They go together, like the obverse and reverse of a coin. When I am buying something from you, if I give you a quarter, it does not matter which side is turned towards you. You accept it because you are sure that the other side is there too. Whatever is required is there. So Light and Consciousness always go together. If one does not live in the transcendental Consciousness, the spiritual heart cannot function properly.

Yes, we can separate the two when we use our human knowledge and wisdom. But when we use our divine wisdom, divine light, divine consciousness, we cannot separate the spiritual heart from the third eye. They are complements, like husband and wife. Since the heart usually is all sweetness and love and the third eye is all power and illumination-light, we can say the heart is the wife and the third eye is the husband. The wife's main qualities are softness, kindness, while the husband's main qualities are knowledge, wisdom and other mental things.

But again, those who are very wise feel that the third eye is also the heart, for what else is the heart except that which gives us satisfaction? And what can give us satisfaction? Only Light! So if Light from the third eye gives us satisfaction, then naturally we are dealing with the heart's quality. And what can give us a constant sense of wisdom? Wisdom comes only when we are deep inside the inmost recesses of our breath, inside our heart where Infinity, Eternity and Immortality play. To possess Infinity as our very own, to possess infinite Light and Bliss eternally as our very own: this is wisdom. So we can say that wisdom comes from the heart. Like this the heart and the third eye go together. Like

Purusha and Prakriti, God as the Father and God as the Mother, the third eye and the heart go together.

Question: If you feel warmth in the region of the heart, is this a sign of the heart centre opening up?

Sri Chinmoy: If you feel heat and the rotation of a disc at the centre of the chest, then it is a sign that the centre is being opened. Doctors say that the physical heart is somewhat to the left of the chest, but the spiritual heart is in the middle of the chest. When the heart centre actually opens, its joy and delight will spread to the whole body so that you cannot actually say that it is located at any specific point.

Question: Do you recommend the use of any special mantra?

Sri Chinmoy: I prefer to advise my disciples to meditate, but I have given mantras to a few of them. Each mantra offers a particular result. While using a mantra, we invoke a certain aspect of God or a certain cosmic god to give us Peace,

Light, Bliss or something else that we want or need. But if we can meditate well for ten or fifteen minutes, this serves the same purpose because we enter into the infinite expanse of Peace, Light and Bliss, where our soul can drink whatever it needs or wants.

When aspirants cannot enter into their deepest meditation because the mind is restless, this is their opportunity to utilise a mantra. "Supreme", "AUM" or "God" can be repeated by anyone for a few minutes before he actually starts his meditation. The mantra should be repeated slowly and aloud.

If you want quick results in your inner spiritual life, you should repeat a mantra every day without fail, for at least half an hour: fifteen minutes in the morning and fifteen minutes in the evening. There can be no mantra more powerful than the mother of all mantras, AUM.

Question: What is the significance of the Gayatri mantra?

Sri Chinmoy: In India we have many mantras. In the Gita, Sri Krishna says that the Gayatri mantra is the best of all the mantras. Its meaning is: "We meditate on the transcendental glory of the Deity Supreme, who is inside the heart of the earth, inside the life of the sky, and inside the soul of the Heaven. May He stimulate and illumine our minds." It is said that if one can recite this special mantra one hundred thousand times, then all his wishes will be fulfilled. Any desire, any aspiration, no matter how mighty, will be fulfilled.

Question: Can you please tell us about a few other mantras?

Sri Chinmoy: The goddess Kali is the Mother of both infinite Power and infinite Compassion. Her seed name or seed form, her mantra, is kring. When she is invoked through her mantra she must be invoked in a powerful way. If you can repeat kring most soulfully and powerfully for just fifteen days, you will see power and fire all around you. This fire will not burn anybody but people will notice it because it will arouse them from their comatose drowsiness.

Some of you have a great fondness for Lord

Krishna. You can invoke him by chanting kling most sweetly. That is his mantra or seed sound.

If you are physically weak, if your physical constitution is not satisfactory, if you chant:

Tejohasi tejomayi dhehi
Viryamasi viryam mayi dhehi
Valam masi valam mayi dhehi

sincerely and soulfully, in a week's time you will see a change for the better in your health. It means:

I pray for dynamic energy;
I pray for dynamic virility;
I pray for indomitable physical strength.

In this world some people are poor while others rich. Some people are desperately in need of money to make both ends meet. Some years ago, a disciple of mine was having tremendous financial difficulties. I gave her a particular mantra:

Ya Devi sarvabhutesu

Meditation

Ratna rupena sangsthita
Nastasvai namastvai
Namastvai namo namah

and in thirteen days she came to me and said that her finances had tremendously improved. The meaning of this mantra is:

> I bow and bow and again I bow to the Supreme Goddess who resides in all human beings in the form of material wealth and prosperity.

Many people have used this mantra in India. In her case it took only thirteen days for the mantra to accomplish its purpose. In someone else's case it may take three months or just three days. This particular mantra has tremendous power, but it is effective only for bringing material wealth.

If you want to remain in supreme Ecstasy and Delight all the time, then you will have to chant this particular mantra:

Anandadd hy eva khalv imani bhutani
  jayante,

Anandena jatani jivanti,
Anandam prayantyabhisam visanti.

We all need Infinity. If Infinity is the particular object of your aspiration, if you want to have infinite Consciousness within and without, then the mantra that you have to practise is:

Purnam adah, purnam idam, purnat
  purnam udacyate.
Purnasya purnam adaya purnam
  evavasisyate.

Question: What happens when we chant AUM?

Sri Chinmoy: A Sanskrit word or syllable has a special significance and creative power. When we chant AUM, what actually happens is that we bring down Peace and Light from above and create a universal harmony within and without us. When we repeat AUM, both our inner and our outer beings become inspired and surcharged with divine Light and aspiration. AUM has no equal. AUM has infinite Power. Just by repeating AUM, we can realise God.

When you chant AUM, try to feel that God is climbing up and down within you. Hundreds of seekers in India have realised God simply by repeating AUM. AUM is the symbol of God, the Creator.

No matter how grave one's sin is, if one chants AUM a few times from the depth of one's heart, the omnipotent Compassion of God will forgive and redeem the victim. In the twinkling of an eye, the power of AUM transforms darkness into Light, ignorance into knowledge and death into Immortality.

Question: How are we actually supposed to chant AUM?

Sri Chinmoy: There are various ways to chant AUM. When we chant AUM with tremendous soul's power, what we actually do is enter into the cosmic vibration where the creation is in perfect harmony and where the cosmic Dance is being danced by the Absolute. If we chant AUM soulfully, we become one with the cosmic Dance; we become one with God the Creator, God the Preserver and God the Transformer. All that

God has within and without, AUM can offer to us, because AUM is at once the Life, the Body and the Breath of God. This is what an Indian seeker or an Indian spiritual Master feels when he chants AUM.

If you get an attack on the emotional vital plane and wrong thoughts, wrong ideas, wrong vibrations enter into you, repeat AUM or the name of the Supreme as fast as possible. Do not chant slowly. When you are trying to cleanse your mind of impurities you must chant as if you were running to catch a moving train.

When you do japa, do not prolong your chanting too much. If you prolong the syllable AUM, you won't have the time to chant five hundred or six hundred times. Just say the syllable in a normal but soulful way so that you will get the vibration.

I know that some of you repeat AUM and "Supreme" at home. It is wonderful that you practise this, but please practise it aloud, not silently. Let the sound of the mantra vibrate even in your physical ears and permeate your entire body.

Meditation

Question: Before beginning meditation and concentration, I was wondering if there should be a specific manner of breathing.

Sri Chinmoy: We have a traditional system of controlled breathing in India which is called pranayama. Prana is the vital energy, the life-breath; yama means control. Pranayama is the control of the life-breath. The very first exercise you can practise is to repeat once, as you breathe in, the name of God, the Supreme, the Christ, or whomever you adore. Or if your Master has given you a mantra, you can repeat that. This breath does not have to be long or deep. Then hold your breath and repeat the same name four times. And when you breathe out, repeat two times the name or mantra that you have chosen. You inhale for one count, hold your breath for four counts, and exhale for two counts, inwardly repeating the sacred name. If you simply count the numbers – one-four-two – you do not get any vibration, any inner feeling. But when you say the name of God, immediately God's divine qualities – Purity, Peace, Love, Bliss and many others – enter into you. Then when you hold your breath, these divine qualities rotate inside you, entering into all your impurities, obscurities, imperfections and limitations. And when you breathe out, these same divine qualities carry away all your undivine, unprogressive, destructive qualities.

The beginner starts with a one-four-two count. When he becomes mature in his breathing, he will be able to do it in a count of four-sixteen-eight: breathing in for four counts, holding the breath for sixteen, and breathing out for eight. But this has to be done very gradually. Some people do it even more. They do an eight-thirty-two-sixteen count, but this is not for the beginner.

Another thing you can try is alternate breathing. This is done by pressing the right nostril with the thumb and taking in a long breath through the left nostril. As you breathe in you repeat God's Name only once. Then you hold your breath for four counts, repeating God's Name. And finally you release your right nostril, press your left nostril with your fourth finger, and release your breath through to the count of two – that is, two repetitions of God's Name. Then you do it the opposite way, starting with the left nostril pressed closed. In this system, when you breathe in, it does not have to be done quietly. Even if you make a noise there is no harm. But of course, these exercises should not be done in public or where other people are trying to meditate in silence. You should not practise one-four-two breathing for more than four or five minutes, and you should not do alternate breathing more than three times. If you do it twenty or forty or fifty times, heat will rise from the base of your spine and enter into your head, creating tension and a headache. It is like eating too much. Eating is good, but if you eat voraciously, it will upset your stomach. This heat acts the same way. If you draw it up beyond your capacity, then instead of giving you a peaceful mind, it will give you an arrogant, destructive, turbulent mind. When you have developed your inner capacity, you can do this alternate breathing for ten or fifteen minutes.

Pranayama is a traditional yogic discipline with many serious, complicated breathing exercises. For these, ten minutes or fifteen minutes or half an hour of practice is good. But pranayama is dangerous if you do not have a teacher to guide you at every step. If you do the exercises improperly, you may develop tuberculosis. Many people in India have contracted this disease because they practise pranayama without proper guidance. But these exercises that I am telling you about – the one-four-two count and alternate nostril breathing – are very simple and, at the same time, effective. They will never harm your lungs.

Question: How can I purify my mind so that I can have a good meditation?

Sri Chinmoy: In your case, the best thing to do is to feel every day for a few minutes that you have no mind. Say, "I have no mind, I have no mind. What I have is the heart." Then after some time, say, "No, I don't have the heart. What I have is the soul."

You have to know that the mind is almost always impure, bringing in dark and bad thoughts. Even when it is not doing this, it is still a victim to doubt, jealousy, hypocrisy, fear and all that. All negative things first attack the mind. You may reject them for a minute, but the next minute they knock at your mind's door again. This is the nature of the mind.

But the heart is much, much purer, because affection, love, devotion, surrender and other divine qualities are already in the heart. Even if you have fear or jealousy in the heart, the good qualities of the heart will still come forward. But again, the heart is not totally pure because the vital being is around the heart. The lower vital, situated near the navel, tends to come up and touch the heart centre. It tries to make the heart impure by its influence and proximity. But at least the heart is not like the mind, which is always opening its door to impure ideas.

Even better than the heart is the soul. Here there is no impurity. The soul is all Purity, Light, Bliss and Divinity. When you say, "I have no mind," this does not mean that you are becoming an animal again. Far from it! You are only saying, "I don't care for this mind, which is bringing me so much impurity and torturing me so much." When you say, "I have the heart," you feel that the heart has some purity. But when you say, "I have the soul," you are flooded with purity. Then, after some time, you have to go deeper and farther and not only say, "I have the soul," but "I am the soul." The moment you say, "I am the soul," and you meditate on this truth, your soul's infinite purity will enter into your heart. Then from the heart, the infinite purity of your soul will enter into the mind. In this way you will purify your mind and your heart and you will be able to have a wonderful meditation every day.

Question: How is it possible to keep one's mind from having any thoughts?

Sri Chinmoy: In the beginning, unless one is very spiritually advanced, it is really impossible for one not to have thoughts. But if you continue to meditate for a few months or a few years, then you will see that it is quite possible to enter into thoughtless meditation. For the time being you should do japa. You should repeat the name of your spiritual Master, if you have one, or of whomever you worship, or of God, let us say. Just repeat, "Supreme, Supreme, Supreme..." continuously. It is true that your mind, your brain, is operating when you do this repetition. But if you continue it for ten minutes most soulfully, then you will see that you are no longer the doer. This word has become spontaneous in your life. It becomes like a passing train, and you are simply riding on that train. This word that is repeating in you is not a thought at that time. It is a reality. Thought binds you, but this reality does not bind. This reality only takes you to your destined goal.

Start with a thought, with an idea, with a concept of Truth, with God. After fifteen minutes or half an hour the thought has played its role. Then you spontaneously go beyond thought and identify yourself with some reality. At that time the mental formation of any thought or idea ceases. Only Reality – God the Reality or whomever you have chosen as the object of your adoration – remains. And this Reality takes you, carries you to your Goal.

Question: How can one recognise a God-realised spiritual Master?

Sri Chinmoy: When you are with a God-realised Master, consciously or unconsciously you are bound to feel some Peace, some Light, some Bliss, some Power, because it is his very nature to radiate these things. He is not showing off; it is spontaneous, as the very nature of a flower is to emit fragrance. Every day you come in contact with thousands of people, but you do not get this from any of them.

A Master's outer body may be very ugly, but in his eyes you will see all divine qualities. And if his eyes are closed, you may observe nothing outwardly, but deep inside yourself you will feel an inner joy that you have never felt before. You have felt joy before, true, but the inner thrill that you will get the moment you stand before a real spiritual Master for the first time can never be described. And if the Master is your own Master, then the joy will be infinitely greater.

You are bound to feel all kinds of divine qualities in the spiritual Master, provided you have aspiration. Otherwise, you may sit in front of the spiritual Master, talk to him, have all kinds of intimate friendship with him, but you will get nothing. It is your aspiration that permits you to receive all the divine qualities of the Master. If you have no aspiration, no matter what the Master has, he will not be able to give it to you.

Also, when you speak to a real Master, your own sincerity has to come forward. This does not mean that you will always express your sincerity. You may tell lies in spite of the fact that your sincerity is pushing you, compelling you to tell the truth. But when you are with a spiritual Master, you at least want to offer your sincerity, although insincerity may come and fight with you and sometimes prevent you.

When you are with a realised Master, you are bound to feel that the Master understands you; and not only that he understands you, but also that he has the capacity to comfort you and help you in your problems. Some people feel that there is nobody on earth to understand them. But, if they are lucky enough to find a person who understands them, they come to know that this person still cannot solve their problems because he does not have inner light, inner wisdom, inner power. A spiritual Master not only understands your problems, but also has the capacity in infinite measure to help you in your needs.

When you stand before a Master, you will feel that he can never be separated from your inner or outer existence. You feel he is your highest part and you want to grow into him. You want to become a perfect part of his highest realisation, for the very divine qualities that you are aspiring for – Light, Joy, Peace, Power – a spiritual Master has in boundless measure.

Question: Is there a specific way to accelerate realisation?

Sri Chinmoy: Yes, there is a specific way, and it is called conscious aspiration. God must come first. There must be no mother, no father, no sister, no brother – nothing else but God, only God. True, we want to see God in humanity, but first we have to see Him face to face. Most of us cry for money, name, fame, material success and prosperity; but we do not cry even for an iota of inner wisdom. If we cry sincerely, devotedly and soulfully for unconditional oneness with our Inner Pilot, then today's man of imperfection will be transformed into tomorrow's God, the perfect Perfection incarnate.

Aspiration, the inner cry, should come from the physical, the vital, the mind, the heart and the soul. Of course, the soul has been aspiring all the time, but the physical, vital, mental and psychic beings have to become consciously aware of this. When we consciously aspire in all parts of our being, we will be able to accelerate the achievement of liberation.

How do we aspire? Through proper concentration, proper meditation and proper contemplation. Aspiration covers both meditation and prayer. In the West, there were many saints who did not care for meditation; they realised God through prayer. He who is praying feels he has an inner cry to realise God, and he who is meditating also feels the need of bringing God's Consciousness right into his being. The difference between prayer and meditation is this:

when I pray, I talk and God listens; and when I meditate, God talks and I listen. When I pray, God has to listen. But when I meditate, when I make my mind calm and quiet, I hear what God has always been saying to me. So both ways are correct.

Conscious aspiration is the first thing we need. Aspiration is all that we have and all that we are. Then consciously we have to offer our aspiration to the Supreme so that we can become one with Him.

Question: When I think of all the failings and undivine qualities in myself and my fellow disciples, illumination seems a million miles away.

Sri Chinmoy: When one is really illumined, one will not see others as imperfect or hopeless human beings. The moment one is illumined, he will feel his real oneness with others and he will see the so-called imperfections of others as an experience God is having in and through them.

Since you are my disciple, I wish to tell you that you see more imperfection, more limitation, more teeming night inside yourself than I can even imagine. To me you are absolutely natural and normal; you are God's child, and you have every opportunity and capacity to realise, manifest and fulfil the Divine here on earth. Illumination is something which you had, but which you now have forgotten; it is not something totally new.

One who really cares for illumination has to feel that he is growing from light to more light to abundant light. If a seeker always feels that he is deep in the sea of ignorance, then I wish to say that he will never, never come out of ignorance, for there is no end to the ignorance-sea. But if one feels that he is growing from an iota of light into the all-pervading, highest Light, then illumination immediately seems easier and more spontaneous.

Question: What can we do during our meditation to transform or to help purify the mind, vital and body?

Sri Chinmoy: To increase the purity of the physical, the vital and the mind during our meditation we should try to feel what purity actually is. If we feel that purity is something liquid, like water, or something weak, elastic, or delicate like a toy, then purity will not increase at all in our physical and our vital. But if we feel that purity is something very powerful, like the strongest man or like an atom bomb, it can create a new life inside us and around us. The atom bomb destroys, but purity has the power of an atom bomb, although in a positive way. Purity can build a strong and solid foundation in our outer life and in our inner life. If we have the feeling that purity is something that will give us a new life, a new world of peace, bliss and dynamic power, then our purity will immediately increase. When we are aware that purity can do much for us, we will value it properly. Then during our meditation purity will enter into us in infinite measure because it will feel that we will give it its proper importance.

Question: What is the most effective way I can attain purity?

Sri Chinmoy: The most effective way to attain purity in your case is through conscious offering of your life-breath to the Supreme. Early in the morning breathe in consciously seven times, and while you breathe in try to feel that you are actually breathing in through your heart and not through your nose. Try to feel that your breath is entering you through your heart centre. And while you are breathing out try to feel that your breath is going up, up to the top of your head and out through the thousand-petaled lotus, the crown centre at the top of your head. If you can feel, and not just imagine, that you are breathing through your heart, immediately purity will enter and start revolving and functioning in you. When purity starts performing its role, impurity from the navel and lower centres travels up and is released.

First the divine soldiers enter and see that the undivine soldiers are there. Then the opponents fight until the divine soldiers push the undivine soldiers up and throw them through the thousand-petaled lotus into the infinite cosmos. It is your mind that unconsciously attracts impurity, so you have to go beyond the mind. You have to carry the impure, undivine soldiers higher, and throw them into something which is beyond the mind. Do this early in the morning and in the evening also, if possible. Then your system is bound to be purified.

Question: How can I maintain my inner strength during my meditation?

Sri Chinmoy: Here the strength is aspiration. During meditation, how can you develop more aspiration in order to go deeper. When you meditate, please do not think of diving deeper. If the mind operates, then you will not be able to go deeper at all. When you feel that you are in a sublime meditation, you will see that the meditation itself has its own power. So you only have to try to surrender to the meditative power within you. At that time do not use your mind. If you are having a profound meditation, then there cannot be any intervention of the mind. The meditation that you are having is the result of the meditative power within you. Just allow this meditative power to play its role. This meditative power will always have a free access to the deeper reality within you. Let it dive deep

Meditation

within if such is the Will of God. But sometimes the meditative power does not enter into the inner or deeper reality because it feels that the entire being is not fully ready. If it enters into the inner reality, there may be a revolt from the outer being. So when you enter into deep meditation, let the force that has already created this sublime meditation flow or grow inside you according to the Will of the Supreme. At that time do not bring your mind forward in order to go deeper or higher. The force that has already shown you its capacity can easily carry you into the deeper parts of your being, but it waits for God's Command or the Command of the Inner Pilot.

When you start meditation, the only thing you do is to make your mind calm and quiet, and then let the meditation do anything it wants to do. You do not act like a doer any more; your responsibility is over. When you have made your mind calm and quiet, your responsibility is totally over. Then you have to let the force, the divine force that is giving you the experience of a good meditation, do whatever else it wants to do in you and for you.

Question: What is the best way to deal with dry periods in one's sadhana? That is, how does one maintain aspiration and good feelings while one experiences a dryness in his meditation?

Sri Chinmoy: When you feel dryness in your meditation, you can easily mix with a friend who is not going through that experience. Take dryness as darkness. When you think of dryness, think of going through the Queens Midtown Tunnel. You know that there will be some light at the end because you have been through the Midtown Tunnel many, many times before. After you enter, for some time you know that there may be no light; but if you have patience you know that you will see light.

In the spiritual life no one is experiencing dryness for the first time. This dryness is fairly common. There are very few seekers who have not gone through it. Some spiritual Masters of the highest order went through dry periods for six or eight months, and sometimes for as long as two years. During a four-year period some of them went through dry periods five or six times.

    This dryness can be avoided by doing only one thing: shedding tears of gratitude. You may say that you are not getting any joy, any satisfaction, anything, from your meditation, so why should you offer gratitude? But you have to offer gratitude just because you are trying to meditate. Who is asking or compelling you to try? Somebody deep within you. The Supreme is asking you to meditate despite the fact that you are going through a dry period. So if you can offer your gratitude, soulful gratitude, tearful gratitude, to the Supreme, the dry period will pass very quickly. Think of the Midtown Tunnel. You can easily cover the distance when the time comes. You know it is only a matter of time. For a short time you will remain in darkness, and then it is bound to end. But if you want to run the fastest, then gratitude is the only answer.

Question: Sometimes when I meditate, I feel that I am about to go through some experience, but nothing happens. What is the cause of that?

Sri Chinmoy: The reason nothing happens is that you have not reached the height, the ultimate. You are just on the verge of it, but you do not quite reach it. It is like lighting a stove. When you turn on the gas, you have to turn it to a certain point before the flame comes. You may come almost to that point, but you stop too soon. If you had turned just a fraction of an inch farther, you would have succeeded.

It is the same with your meditation. If you had gone just a bit higher or deeper, you would have had your experience. But your attention was diverted or something made you pull back instead of going on. Something inside you failed to maintain the same type of aspiration that you had before and then your consciousness fell. It is as if you were climbing up to the highest branch of a mango tree, but all of a sudden somebody called you from below and you forgot about the delicious mango at the top of the tree and you climbed down. This is what it is like when consciousness falls. But if you can maintain your height and not respond to any call from below, then you will reach the Highest, and here you will get the experience.

While you are praying and meditating, imagine that you have a bicycle inside you. When you ride on a bicycle, you have to pedal it all the time. If you don't pedal, you cannot make any progress and you will fall down. While you are meditating you have to aspire all the time; otherwise you will fall. You cannot balance motionless at one point. In the spiritual life movement has to be constant. Either you move forward or you move backward. If you try to remain motionless, the ignorance of the world will pull you right back to your starting point.

While we are aspiring we have to make ourselves conscious at every moment that what we need is not success, but progress, progress, progress. Progress itself is the active form of success. When we start meditating early in the morning, if we think, "Today I have to get the highest experience or I will feel miserable," then we are making a mistake. Right now we are full of ignorance, imperfection, limitation and bondage. But if we remain imperfect, how are we going to be the chosen instruments of God? And if we cannot become instruments of God, then God remains unmanifested. In the morning when we pray, if we cry for our progress, then automatically God will make us His chosen instruments. But if we cry for success, then God may give us the experience which we call success, but He will not utilise us as His instruments because we are already trying to get something from Him. We are demanding that He give us the highest experience of Peace, Light and Bliss, whereas we should be asking only for the opportunity and privilege of being His instrument to serve Him in His own Way.

So I wish to say that if experience is your aim, until you actually reach the height from which you can get the experience, please continue to aspire intensely. But if your aim is only to become an instrument of the Supreme, no matter how high or how deep you go, then you are bound to get all the experiences which God has in store for you, even without climbing up to the top of the tree. Right now it is you who are trying to climb up to a great height in order to get an experience. But it is very easy for God to bring the fruit down and give it to you. He is an expert climber: He can climb up and climb down. So if you can please God, even if you remain at the foot of the tree, God will climb up on your behalf and bring the experience down, if it is His Will that you have it.

Question: How can our imagination be used to help raise our consciousness or improve our meditation?

Sri Chinmoy: First of all, we have to know that imagination is not mental hallucination. If we take imagination as something unproductive, as something that has nothing to do with reality, then imagination will never be reality. If we think that imagination is the South Pole and reality is the North Pole, then it is all useless. We have to take imagination as a reality in another world, in an inner world or a higher world. And that world we have to bring into the world of reality that we are now living in. Imagination is a world of reality which is waiting for revelation and manifestation here in this outer world, which we know as reality.

Inside us are many worlds; imagination is one of these worlds. We have a free access to the world that is around us and before us, whereas we do not have a free access to the worlds that are inside us. So what we have to try to do is bring the world that is inside us into the world that is around us. It is like this: somebody is inside the house and somebody is outside the house. You are friendly with the person who is outside the house. You know him well because most of the time you stay outside. But when you come inside, you see that somebody else is there. You can also make friends with that person and ask him to come out with you and make friends with the person who is staying outside.

So, think of imagination as a reality in its own right which is on another plane of consciousness. That plane of consciousness you are trying to bring to the fore and make one with the plane of consciousness which we call reality. You are trying to establish friendship between the two: between the imagination-world, which is a reality-world in another plane of consciousness, and the reality-world which is the outer plane of consciousness. But this you can do only if you take imagination as a reality in another plane, in its own world.

Imagination plays a most significant role in the spiritual life. Suppose you are not having good meditations, but six months ago you had a very good, powerful, high meditation. What you can do is try to imagine that powerful meditation. Then your imagination will become reality. After fifteen minutes or half an hour, you will get a good meditation. Vivekananda was such a great spiritual figure, yet sometimes for six months at a time he did not have a good meditation. What did he do? He used to imagine a time when he did have a good meditation, and inside his imagination was aspiration. So imagination is very good.

Question: How can I have deeper meditation?

Sri Chinmoy: You can have deeper meditation through constant remembrance of your goal. Always think of your goal as something high, higher, highest. If your goal is not the highest, if your goal is not boundless Peace, boundless Light, boundless Bliss, then your meditation cannot be very deep. Only when you pitch your aim to the highest, do you go high, higher, highest. If you want to be satisfied with only an iota of Peace, Light and Bliss, then you cannot go deeper; you cannot go higher. Always when you meditate, try to bring into your being boundless Peace, Light and Bliss or throw yourself into something infinite, something vast. These qualities will act like a springboard. If you press hard on the springboard, then you jump higher.

In order to have good meditation you should also try to dedicate your life to the right cause. The right cause is to see the divine in others and the divine in yourself all the time. If you can see yourself only as divine, then you are bound to have a deeper meditation. The moment you think of yourself as a bundle of ignorance, as a sea of ignorance, you are taking the wrong way of approaching the truth. Try to see the divine in yourself as often as you can; then automatically your meditation becomes deeper, more

Meditation

illumining and more fulfilling.

Question: After we stop meditating, how can we maintain the level of consciousness we reached during our meditation?

Sri Chinmoy: Here we are all aspiring; that is why our consciousness is elevated. The meeting will last for about half an hour more. Then we shall go home and our consciousness will go down. How can we maintain our present level of consciousness? We can do it through constant remembrance.

After you leave the Centre and go home, you may not retain the same level of aspiration because of some family difficulty or other problems. But even if there is nothing to prevent you from continuing to aspire, your own limited being will not allow you to stay on the top of the tree. You aspire for half an hour with utmost sincerity and then relaxation starts. You feel that you have worked very hard and now you are entitled to rest.

But the spiritual life is not like that. If you want to maintain your standard, if you want to maintain the height of your aspiration, then your aspiration should be flowing constantly. Suppose you have meditated for an hour; then you may not be able to meditate again for another hour or so. It is difficult right now for all of us to meditate for eight hours. But no harm. For half an hour you can easily meditate. Then you can do something which will maintain and preserve your meditation. For the next half-hour you can read spiritual books; then after that you can sing spiritual songs. Then you can go to the house of one of your spiritual brothers or sisters or, if that is not possible, you can call up someone on the phone and speak only about spiritual matters.

Again, you can write about your own experiences in your own way, not with the thought of publishing them but just to help your own consciousness. While you are writing them down, you are perfecting your spiritual nature. For half an hour you can write them down, then you will read what you have written. As soon as you have written down your experiences, you have created something. The creator always wants to enjoy his creation. Look at a gardener

Meditation

when he sees a beautiful rose. First he took great pains to plant a rose bush and tend to it; then after six or seven months when he sees the rose, he deeply appreciates and admires the beautiful flower. Similarly, you also may get joy from reading about your own experiences.

It takes fifteen or twenty minutes for you to eat. During that time try to remember what experiences you had while you were meditating early in the morning. Just imagine them. This imagination is not fantasy or self-deception: it is like charging a battery. You are charging your memory with your achievement, with your spiritual progress. Each time you think about your own experiences, you will be transported back to that time and you will get abundant Peace, Light and Bliss and so forth. So in this way you can always retain your meditation from the early morning and you will be able to maintain your standard until it is time for your next meditation.

But unfortunately people don't do this. We meditate for half an hour or forty-five minutes and immediately we feel that we are tired and exhausted. Then we do so many wrong things.

It is a kind of negative reaction. We feel that we have seen one side of the river and now we want to go to the other shore. But the other shore is unfortunately all darkness. We have to try to remain on the shore that has light. So to preserve our meditation we will do other things which will increase or at least retain the power of the meditation.

During the week we have to go to work. Early in the morning we meditate and elevate our consciousness, but then we spend seven or eight hours at work and we are unfortunately compelled to mix with people who are unaspiring. We are thrown into a world of desire, fear, anxiety, worry and so forth, and our consciousness falls. So what do we do? Please meditate early in the morning and read spiritual books, sing spiritual songs, mix with spiritual people. Then, when you are in the office or involved in some other activity, try to remain in the consciousness of your early morning meditation and other spiritual activities. In your early morning meditation you have gained Peace, Light and Bliss, which is spiritual money. Keep that inside your own heart, which is the safest of all banks. Then, when you enter into the world, when you are in the office where it is all anxiety, worry and desire, you withdraw some of your spiritual wealth. You concentrate on your heart and bring forward a little of the Peace, Light and Bliss which you acquired early in the morning. It is your own wealth and you can use it. In this way you will be able to maintain your spiritual standard and keep your level of consciousness high.

Right now, we have to be very careful and wise in our day-to-day life about how we spend each hour. But a time will come when our life itself will be a continuous flow of aspiration. Now after our meditation we use the mind and think, "Oh, the time has come for me to read some spiritual books." But one day we won't have to make any conscious effort. Our inner being will inspire us to read spiritual books. Right now the inner being is inside, deeply hidden, but we are trying our best, through Yoga, to bring it to the fore.

II

TALKS ON MEDITATION

Meditation

What is meditation?

What is meditation? Meditation is man's self-awakening and God's Self-offering. When man's self-awakening and God's Self-offering meet together, man becomes immortal in his inner consciousness and God becomes fulfilled in the world of manifestation. "Meditation" is a most complicated and most fulfilling word. When we meditate without knowing how to meditate, when we meditate with our mind, it is most complicated. But when we meditate with our inner conviction, with the feeling of divinity within us, it becomes most fulfilling.

Meditation means conscious self-expansion. Meditation means one's conscious awareness of the transcendental Reality. Meditation means the recognition or the discovery of one's own true self. It is through meditation that we transcend limitation, bondage and imperfection. First we face limitations, imperfections and bondage, then we transform them, and afterwards we transcend them.

Meditation is the language of God. Now I am

speaking English and you are able to understand me. If we want to communicate with God, then meditation is the language. It is the common language of man and God. God uses it and we use it. When we go deep within, into the deepest recesses of our hearts, we commune with God through meditation. It is through meditation that we can know that God is both with form and without form, with attributes and without attributes.

Meditation is dynamism on the inner planes of consciousness. If we want to achieve anything, either in our inner life or our outer life, then the help of meditation is of paramount importance. When we meditate, what we actually do is enter into the deeper part of our being. At that time, we are able to bring to the fore the wealth that we have deep within us. Meditation shows us how we can aspire for something and, at the same time, how we can achieve it. It is through meditation that we can enter into an object, a subject, a person, or into Infinity and Eternity. If we practise meditation daily, then we can rest assured that the problems of our life, inner and outer, are solved.

Why do we meditate? We meditate precisely because this world of ours has disappointed us and because failure looms large in our day-to-day life. We want fulfilment. We want joy, peace, bliss and perfection within and without. Meditation is the answer, the only answer.

True meditation can never be done with the mind. Very often we make a mistake when we say that we are meditating in the mind and utilising the mind. Real meditation is done in the psychic being and in the soul. It goes hand in hand with flaming aspiration, the burning flame that wants to climb up to the Highest.

Each soul is running consciously or unconsciously towards the Goal, but those who are running consciously will reach the Goal sooner than those who are still asleep. All human beings without exception will reach God, but through meditation we reach our Goal sooner. We have to know how fast we want to reach our goal. If I want to come to Puerto Rico from New York, I can come by boat, I can take a direct flight, or I can take a plane that stops at various places on the way. It is entirely up to me whether I take a direct route or an indirect route. There are many roads that lead to the Goal, but one road is sure to be shorter than the others. In the spiritual life, it is when we meditate on the heart that we make the fastest progress. Naturally, if we are wise we will take the shortest route. Each second counts.

Real meditation we get from within or from a spiritual Master. We can never get it from books. From books we can get inspiration or an inner approach to the fulfilment of our outer life. But in order to have true meditation we have to go deep within or follow the guidance of a spiritual Master. Each individual must have a meditation of his own. Each one has to follow a particular path. There is collective meditation and, at the same time, there is a specific meditation for each individual. If you are sitting in a group meditating collectively, that is wonderful, but if you want to realise God, then you have to have your own specific method. This specific way of meditating either your soul will tell you or you will get it from someone who can enter into your soul and see its possibilities, someone who can see how your particular soul wants to manifest the divine Truth here on earth. Some souls want to manifest the Divine on earth through Beauty, while other souls want to manifest the Divine through Power, Light or Bliss. You have to know what your soul wants and how your soul wants to take part in the cosmic Play. Only then will your meditation fulfil the Divine within you and the Divine in the rest of humanity.

There are many seekers whose meditation is not fruitful because they are not doing the meditation that is necessary for them. They are not meditating in the right way. When we meditate properly and soulfully, we can eventually expect a bumper crop of realisation. But if we are constantly knocking at the wrong door and meditating in a wrong way, then we are wasting our time.

Again, I wish to say that in the process of evolution no human being will remain unrealised. It may take millennia, but each individual soul will realise God. Meditation tells us that yesterday's message is to be rejected, today's message is to be accepted and tomorrow's message is to be embraced. What is yesterday's message? Yesterday's message is frustration, imperfection and limitation. If we look backward we can immediately feel and realise that we were unfulfilled, we were imperfect, we were swimming in the sea of bondage. Today's message tells us to go deep within and see the face of reality. It makes us feel that the outer life can easily be transcended and that we can see God face to face. And tomorrow's message is that we can easily claim Divinity as our very own on the strength of our soulful aspiration and meditation.

Meditation

Individual meditation

There are quite a few ways to meditate, but no matter whose path you follow, mine or somebody else's, there is a general rule: you cannot allow your mind to be restless or agitated. You have to try to make the mind calm and quiet, like the bottom of the Pacific Ocean. This advice all the spiritual Masters will give.

How will you make the mind calm and quiet? The mind has its own power, but right now your determination does not have the same degree of power. The mind's power is now stronger than your present eagerness to meditate. But if you can get help from your heart, then easily you will be able to control the mind. The heart gets constant assistance from the soul; and the soul has all light and all power. If you take help from the heart, then you won't allow all kinds of silly rubbish – unlit, undivine thoughts – to enter into your mind. I always tell my disciples to begin their meditation by repeating the word "Supreme" a few times. The Supreme is our eternal Guru: my Guru, your Guru, everybody's

Guru. I am representing the Supreme only for my disciples, who think that I can be of service to them. There are other Masters who are representing the Supreme for their disciples. So think of the Supreme and repeat the word "Supreme" a few times early in the morning. If you can chant "Aum" soulfully, it will also help you during your meditation.

Also, you have to take help from the outer world. If you take a shower or a proper bath in the morning, it adds to your meditation. If you keep flowers in front of your shrine and burn incense and candles, it will help you. When you look at a candle flame, immediately you are inspired, and this inspiration has to enter into your aspiration. In this way the outer flame helps the inner flame.

You people may say, "I don't know how to meditate." But I wish to say that once you become a disciple and enter into my Boat, then it is the problem of the Boatman to take you to the Golden Shore. After you are safely seated in the Boat, you can lie down, you can sing, you can dance, you can do anything. But first you have to enter into the Boat. Occasionally I have given instruction outwardly to some of my disciples who needed it. But to most I don't give individual meditations: each one is allowed to meditate in his own way. When I accept a disciple, I concentrate on his soul and bring the soul forward. Then I give some inner meditation to the soul. At that time, the disciple is bound to receive my inner instruction. But if the disciple can consciously create a pure vibration and keep a sincere attitude, then it is easier for his soul to remain at the fore and to receive everything from me. In the early days I was very liberal in giving the disciples individual meditations. I had one disciple who never got satisfactory results from the meditations I gave her. She would come back after I gave her one meditation and ask me to please give her another one. Then I would give her another and she would come begging me for still another. That particular disciple used to go to all sorts of other spiritual Masters and she used to go to movies, parties and nightclubs. Then she would complain that the meditation I had given her didn't work!

What could I do? The first one I gave should have been effective. Only out of compassion I kept giving her different meditations. Finally she accused me of not having any inner vision.

If you feel that you are inwardly drawn towards me but you have not got an individual meditation, do not worry. The best type of meditation comes when you enter into my consciousness by looking at my Transcendental picture and throwing yourself into me. Just concentrate on this picture of me when I am at one with the Supreme and enter into me through the forehead, where my Eye of Vision is located – the Eye which sees the present, past and future. You also have this Third Eye, but in your case it is still veiled. If you find it difficult to enter into my Third Eye, then try to breathe in slowly and steadily and imagine that I am also breathing rhythmically with you. You can be a few feet away or as close as possible to my picture, but try to feel that we are breathing at the same time.

When you meditate on my picture, you have to try to throw yourself into me with your utmost aspiration. Then I can take full responsibility for your meditation. When you enter into me, you should not feel that you are entering into a foreign element or a foreign person, but that you are entering into something which is your true self, your own highest part. But sometimes you may look at the ocean of Light inside me and feel, "Oh my God, if I enter into the ocean, then I will be drowned. I will be overpowered, destroyed." Here the Light is trying to enter into you in abundant measure and you are trying to hide. But what have you done? Have you committed any crime? Only if you have done something wrong will you try to hide. You have to know that the light will not expose you: it only wants to illumine you. The more light that comes, the sooner you will be illumined. But if you feel fear, then it is better for you not to enter into me. Instead, you should allow me to enter into you. You will say, "Let the ocean come into me in one very, very small drop, or let just a few drops of its water and Light enter into me." This is another way. It all depends on your strength and receptivity and how much of my spiritual food you can eat. If you feel that you are strong enough to swim in my sea of Light and Bliss, then enter into me. If you have great inner strength, then enter into me. Otherwise, let me enter into you.

When you look at my Transcendental picture, try to feel that this person you are seeing is your very own. You have a husband or wife, you have children, and now you can add one more person to your family. You have to feel also that here is someone who is not only your own for this life, but who will be your own forever. If you feel your oneness with me, if you feel that I am not a foreigner but a member of your own family, then automatically you will try to mix with me and your consciousness, your soul, will try to mix with mine. This very mixing is called meditation.

When you meditate on me or on my Transcendental picture, you are becoming one with me. If you look at a tree, you become one with the consciousness of the tree. If you look at a flower, you become one with the fragrance of the flower. Similarly, if you look at my Transcendental picture, you become one with my inner divinity and reality. If you are sincere, at that time you get Peace, Light and Bliss in boundless measure. That is real meditation. But this is only for seekers who want to follow my path.

Those present here who are not my disciples may be thinking that it is the height of folly for my disciples to meditate on my picture. Perhaps they feel that I am proud, conceited and shameless because I allow them to admire that picture. But I can assure you – as my devoted disciples who have faith in me know – that my Transcendental picture does not represent my physical body. It does not represent me, Chinmoy Kumar Ghose. The picture was taken when I was in my highest consciousness; and in that consciousness I am totally one with the Supreme. So that picture represents the Supreme for each seeker who has accepted me as his Guru. When my disciples concentrate, when they meditate in front of that picture, they feel that they are meditating in front of the Supreme.

Those who are my real disciples, dedicated disciples, need not concentrate on anybody's photograph except mine. I tell them to first look at my whole face and then gradually, gradually to try to concentrate on my Third Eye. Whatever they want, if they want a vision or anything else, then my Transcendental picture will give it to them. It has infinite Light, infinite Peace, infinite Bliss; everything it has in infinite measure.

Your Guru is the farmer. He is all the time cultivating the field, which is you. Now if you don't allow him to cultivate, if you consciously or unconsciously turn to somebody else, then you are nowhere near the Goal. It is not that I will be jealous if you put up a picture of some god or goddess in your room; I am very fond of the gods and goddesses. But if I am to carry you to the Golden Shore, then you have to be in my Boat. For concentration, for meditation, for contemplation, for everything you have to come to me and I have to come to you.

If you have a beautiful picture of a god or goddess, you can use this picture for inspiration. But if you concentrate on it, meditate on it, there will be tremendous, tremendous confusion. One day you look at this picture and pray, the

Meditation

following day you will pray to another goddess, the third day to somebody else and the fourth day to me. Then I will be helpless. So I always tell my dearest disciples to stick to me as I stick to them all the time. You can keep other pictures for inspiration if you want to, but not for anything else.

My true disciples and all those who believe in me should have this picture in their meditation room. Also, they should carry a small one in their wallets so that they can look at it on different occasions during the day and when they are about to make important decisions. This way they can easily come in contact with my highest consciousness at any moment. You have become my disciples precisely because you have felt something in me: some Peace, Light, Bliss or Power. Some divine quality of mine you have felt. Also, you feel that this divine quality can easily enter into you. I have all kinds of disciples: first-class, second, third, fourth, fifth, sixth and seventh-class disciples. But, no matter which category you belong to, if you can meditate or concentrate on my Transcendental picture, then you are bound to enter into my inner divine consciousness.

Love, devotion and surrender are the cornerstones of my philosophy because I feel that they make up the true sunlit path which can lead the aspirant to the Goal very fast. If you want to enter into my consciousness while looking at my picture, the best approach is that of love, devotion and surrender. If you want to concentrate and meditate on my picture and offer your heart's love, devotion and surrender, then my highest is also your highest.

I tell my disciples that it is always best to keep the eyes open while meditating. Otherwise, you will keep your eyes closed and then you may think that you are having a wonderful meditation when perhaps you have actually made friends with sleep. Instead of making friends with sleep, you should make an eternal friendship with my divine consciousness. Always keep your eyes open and meditate on my picture. Then you will feel my presence inside your heart. When someone becomes my disciple he has to feel my presence in his heart and also his

Meditation

own presence in my heart. When a disciple meditates on my picture, it automatically helps him in concentrating on the heart. And if he concentrates on his heart, automatically he will feel my presence there.

In the beginning please do not be disturbed if you cannot meditate well. God alone knows how many years one must practise in order to become a very good pianist. If an accomplished pianist thinks of what his standard was when he first began to play, he will laugh. It is through gradual progress that he has achieved his present height in his music. In the spiritual life also, in the beginning do not worry if you find it difficult to meditate. Do not pull or push. Ten minutes early in the morning is enough.

If you meditate every day, you will be able to make progress in your inner life. Again, you have to feel that every day you cannot eat the most delicious meal. Today you may eat most delicious food and then for three or four days you may eat very simple food. As long as you are eating and getting nourishing food, you know that you are sustaining your body. So, if you have a good meditation one day and then the following day you do not have a good meditation, do not feel miserable. In the spiritual life your business is to meditate, meditate. If one day you can't meditate very well or according to your satisfaction, please feel that some other day the Lord Supreme will again give you the opportunity, inspiration and aspiration to meditate extremely well. But if you are disturbed or irritated, then you will lose the opportunity to meditate well in the future. The best thing is to be very calm, quiet and steady in your spiritual life. Then definitely you will be able to meditate well and your meditation will be of the highest order.

Again, you have to know that meditation is not just sitting in front of your shrine. No! When you work for me and you think of me while working, that is one of the best forms of meditation. When you work for me, my consciousness enters into you and you remain in my consciousness. One of the best forms of meditation, dynamic meditation, is soulful dedication – not to sit and go into trance, but to work for me devotedly. If you want to follow somebody else's path, that person may give you different instructions, but this is one of the ways my disciples meditate.

Once you have entered into the spiritual life, at every moment you are dealing with consciousness. When you use the word "consciousness", immediately you will see inside you a vast ocean or a vast sky. The word itself has that capacity. My disciples should feel that the infinite consciousness is within me. My name, Chinmoy, means "full of divine consciousness". When you think of me during the day, feel that you are thinking only of consciousness. When you think of consciousness, you are bound to feel an expansion; the very reality of consciousness is to expand.

When you think of me, see if you can visualise or feel a vast expanse right in front of you. If on the physical plane or on the material plane the earth atmosphere gives you a sense of vastness, try to imagine it when you think of me. When you look at the ocean, you will see an expanse of water. Water means consciousness. When you look at the sky, immediately you feel an infinite expanse of blue, of vastness. So you can expand your heart by looking at the ocean and feeling that the ocean is representing my consciousness and your heart is becoming one with it. Or you can look at the sky early in the morning just for a few seconds and feel that there your heart has become one with my consciousness.

I am a spiritual teacher, but I am not the only spiritual teacher on earth; there are a few others. If you follow my path, I will be able to offer light to your soul and your soul will be able to guide you and show you how to meditate. If you study my writings, if you come to our Centre meetings regularly and concentrate on my picture, if you work for me devotedly, then you will learn how to meditate. But if you follow someone else's path, naturally that teacher will teach you how to meditate in his own specific way.

Meditation

The supreme secret of meditation

Meditation is man's thirst for the Infinite Real, Eternal Real and Absolute Real. The secret of meditation is to achieve conscious and constant oneness with God. The secret supreme of meditation is to feel God as one's very own, and finally to realise God for God's sake, Him to reveal and Him to fulfil.

Meditation has to be practised spontaneously, soulfully and correctly. If it is not, dark doubt will blight your mind and utter frustration will steal into your heart. And you will probably find your whole existence thrown into the depths of a yawning chasm.

For meditation you need inspiration. Scriptures can supply you with inspiration. To buy a spiritual book takes ten seconds. To read that book takes a few hours. To absorb that book takes a few years. And to live the truths thereof may take not only a whole lifetime, but a few incarnations.

For meditation you need aspiration. The presence, physical or spiritual, of a spiritual teacher can awaken your sleeping aspiration. He can easily and will gladly do it for you. Aspiration: this is precisely what you need in order to reach your journey's goal. You don't have to worry about your realisation. Your aspiration will take care of it.

Meditation nourishes your self-discipline. Self-discipline strengthens your meditation. Meditation purifies your heart. And in a pure heart alone looms large the Godward march of human life. One may know what proper meditation is. One may even practise it, since that is what the divine nature in man needs. But the result or fulfilment of meditation transcends all human understanding, for it is measureless, limitless, infinite.

Meditation tells you only one thing: God is. Meditation reveals to you only one truth: yours is the vision of God.

To my extreme sorrow, some of you in the West have grave misconceptions about meditation. You feel that the acme of meditation is fortune-telling or miracle-mongering. Fortune-telling does not rhyme with meditation. Miracle-mongering does not rhyme with meditation, either. But realisation perfectly rhymes with meditation. Liberation soulfully rhymes with meditation. Do you really want to realise God? Do you really want God's Infinite Light, Peace and Bliss? If so, you should keep millions and millions of miles away from fortune-tellers and miracle-mongers. If you think that they inspire you, then you are mistaken. Go deep within and you will discover that they have just aroused your idle, eyeless and fruitless curiosity. Curiosity is not spirituality. And secretly and consciously the fortune-tellers and miracle-mongers have offered you something more: temptation. Temptation is the harbinger of destruction. It is here that the divine mission of your life – unsuccessful, unfulfilled – comes to an end. Let us be on the alert. I urge you not to confuse your heart's genuine meditation with fortune-telling and miracle-mongering. Don't waste your time. Your time is precious. Your meditation is priceless. Your achievement shall be the treasure of timeless Eternity, measureless Infinity and deathless Immortality. Don't wait. All things come to him who waits, except the realisation that today embodies and the liberation that now reveals.

Meditation is our soul's cry for our life's perfect perfection. Perfection has not yet dawned on earth, but one day it will. Perfection is the ideal of human life. To quote Swami Vivekananda: "None of us has yet seen an ideal human being, and yet we are told to believe in him. None of us has yet seen an ideally perfect man, and yet without that ideal we cannot progress."

Meditation alone can give birth to perfection. Meditation carries us beyond the frustration of the senses, beyond the limitation of the reasoning mind. And, finally, meditation can present us with the breath of perfection.

The ultimate aim of meditation is to realise the Supreme. The Katha Upanishad has a spiritual message to offer to the world. This message is an inner message.

> Higher than the senses are the objects
> of the senses.

> Higher than the objects of the senses
> is the mind.
> Higher than the mind is the intellect.
> Higher than the intellect is the Great
> Self.
> Higher than the Great Self is the
> Unmanifest.
> Higher than the Unmanifest is the
> Person.
> Higher than the Person there is
> nothing at all.
> That is the goal. That is the highest
> course.

Indeed, the Person is the Supreme Himself. On the strength of our highest and deepest meditation we unfailingly gain free access to the Supreme.

At the beginning of our spiritual journey, we feel that meditation is self-effort and perspiration. At the end of our journey's close, we realise that meditation is God's Grace, His Compassion Infinite.

The price is never right. Before realisation, it is too high. After realisation, it is too low.

Sri Chinmoy

Meditation

Meditation is invocation. We invoke God's Presence. God's Presence is satisfaction.

Meditation is an act of inner listening. We listen to the dictates of God. When we listen soulfully, devotedly, unreservedly and unconditionally, we derive satisfaction in boundless measure.

Meditation is acceptance. It is the acceptance of life within us, without us and all around us. Acceptance of life is the beginning of human satisfaction. Transformation of life is the culmination of divine satisfaction.

Meditation is self-giving. We give what we have and what we are. To the finite reality we give what we have. To the infinite Reality we give what we are. What we have is concern. This concern we offer to the finite. What we are is willingness. This willingness we offer to the Infinite.

Assurance we offer to the earth-reality. Acknowledgement we offer to the Heaven-Reality. To the earth-reality we offer our constant assurance that we are undoubtedly and unmistakably for the earth-reality, for the transformation and illumination of the earth-reality. To the Heaven-Reality we offer our most sincere acknowledgement of the supreme fact that we are of the Heaven-Reality, that our source is the Heaven-Reality.

Meditation and prayer are two aspects of one and the same soulful reality. The Eastern world is fond of meditation. The Western world is fond of prayer. Both prayer and meditation lead us to the selfsame Goal. Meditation and prayer are like brother and sister; they are divine twins. We can say that prayer is the female and meditation is the male. Prayer says to meditation, "Look, brother, there is something high above. Let us cry and fly, fly and cry, and there above we shall get everything that we have been longing for." Meditation says to prayer, "Look, sister, there is something deep within us. Let us dive deep within and we are sure to get everything that we have been longing for from time immemorial. Let us dive deep within."

Sri Krishna meditated. His meditation-power

has taught us many things. But the most important thing it has taught us is this: Truth will ultimately prevail; the justice-light of Truth will one day inundate the entire earth-consciousness.

Lord Buddha meditated. His meditation has taught us that this human life of suffering will, without fail, one day come to an end. The excruciating pangs that each human being undergoes will one day come to an end, and human suffering will be transformed into divine ecstasy.

The Saviour Christ prayed. His prayer has taught us many sublime, soulful and fruitful lessons. It has offered us the message of divinity in its tangible form. But his most essential teaching is that the Kingdom of Heaven is within us. This Kingdom of Heaven is God's Creation, God's Vision and God's Reality. God's Transcendental Vision and God's Universal Reality are within this Kingdom of Heaven.

Let us meditate devotedly, soulfully, unreservedly and unconditionally. From our meditation we shall discover the supreme truth that as we need God, even so, God needs us. We need Him constantly to reach our own highest height. He needs us constantly to manifest His own deepest depth.

Sri Chinmoy

Meditation

Meditation is the language of God. When you and I speak English, we are able to understand one another. If you want to communicate with God, then meditation is the language that you must speak. It is the common language of man and God. God uses it and man uses it. When you go deep within, into the deepest recesses of your heart, you commune with God through meditation.

Thinking has nothing to do with meditation. Even reflection, which is a quiet kind of introspective thinking, is far from the disciplined vastness of meditation. The moment you start thinking, you play with limitation and bondage. Your thoughts, no matter how sweet or delicious at the moment, are painful, venomous and destructive in the long run because they limit and bind you. In the thinking mind there is no reality. One moment you are building a castle and the following moment you are breaking it. The mind has its purpose, but in the spiritual life you have to go far above the mind

Meditation

where there is eternal peace, eternal knowledge and eternal light. When you go beyond thinking with the help of your aspiration and meditation, only then can you see and enjoy God's Reality and God's Vision together.

Sri Chinmoy

Meditation: an introduction

Why do we meditate? We meditate precisely because we need something. And what is that something? That something is the conscious feeling of our oneness with the Supreme. This need must be spontaneous, genuine and soulful.

Let me start with the ABC of meditation. The best way to meditate is to sit cross-legged on a small cushion or rug. The spine and the neck must be kept erect. If it is not possible for some of you to sit that way, then please try, if you are sitting on a chair, to sit with your entire back straight and erect.

If you want to meditate at home, please try to keep a sacred place, a corner of your room, absolutely pure and sanctified. And please wear clean and light clothes. In order to have the utmost purity, it is extremely helpful to bathe before meditation, but if you are unable to take a bath or shower before sitting down to meditate, you should at least wash your face and your feet. If possible, please burn incense at the time of your meditation, and place one flower, any flower, in front of you.

When you are meditating at home, if it is possible, please meditate all alone. This rule does not apply to husband and wife if they have the same spiritual Master; they can meditate together. Also close spiritual friends who understand each other thoroughly in their inner lives can meditate together. Otherwise it is not advisable to meditate with others. In our Centre, however, the disciples should and do meditate collectively, since collective meditation is of paramount importance also. But for individual daily meditation, I feel it is better if one meditates in one's own room, privately, even in secret.

It is helpful during your meditation to have in front of you a picture of the Christ or some other spiritually beloved figure whom you regard as your Master. Those who are my disciples will have a picture of me taken when I was in my own highest Consciousness. There I am absolutely One with my Inner Pilot. I tell my disciples, when they meditate on the picture, "Either you enter into me or allow me to enter into you. Then I shall meditate on your behalf."

Sometimes people ask me what they should do if they are restless and don't have a good meditation. If any of you find it difficult to meditate on a particular day, then do not try to force yourself. If you are my disciple, just look at my picture – at my eyes, or my forehead, or even at my nose. Just look. If you belong to someone else, or if you have no Guru, but you do have a picture of a peaceful scene to concentrate on, please concentrate on that and do not try to force yourself to meditate. Then, when you get up for your daily work, do not feel miserable that you could not meditate. If you feel that your Inner Being is displeased with you or if you are displeased with yourself, then you are making a great mistake. If you cannot meditate on a particular day, try to give the responsibility for this to me, if you are my disciple, or to the Supreme. If you feel sorry or despondent, the progress that you made yesterday or the day before will be nullified.

In order to meditate properly, purity is of utmost importance. How can we be pure? To try to control our senses and conquer our passions cannot bring us the purity we want and need. The hungry lion that lives in our senses and the hungry tiger that lives in our passions will not leave us by the mere repetition of the thought, "I shall control my senses and conquer my passions." This approach is of no avail.

What we must do is to fix our mind on God. To our utter amazement, our lion and tiger, now tamed, will leave us of their own accord when they see that we have become too poor to feed them. But, as a matter of fact, we don't become poor in the least. On the contrary, we become infinitely stronger and richer, for God's Will energises our body, mind and heart. To fix our body, mind and heart on the Divine is the right approach. The closer we are to the Light, the further we are from the Darkness.

Purity does not come all at once. It takes time. We must dive deep and lose ourselves with implicit faith in contemplation on God. We need not go to purity. Purity will come to us. And purity does not come alone. It brings an everlasting joy with it. This divine joy is the sole purpose of our life. God reveals Himself fully and manifests Himself unreservedly only when we have this inner joy.

The world gives us desires. God gives us prayers. The world gives us bondage. God gives us freedom: freedom from limitation, freedom from ignorance.

We are the player. We can play either football or cricket. We have a free choice. Similarly, it is we who can choose to play with either purity or impurity. The player is the master of the game and not vice versa.

Let nothing perturb us. Let our body's impurity remind us of our heart's spontaneous purity. Let our outer finite thoughts remind us of our inner infinite Will. Let our mind's teeming imperfections remind us of our soul's limitless Perfection.

The present-day world is full of impurity. It seems that purity is a currency from another world. It is hard to obtain this purity, but once we get it, peace is ours, success is ours.

Let us face the world. Let us take life as it comes. Our Inner Pilot is constantly vigilant. The undercurrents of our inner and spiritual

Meditation

life will always flow on unnoticed, unobstructed, unafraid.

God may be unknown but He is not unknowable. Our prayers and meditation lead us to that unknown. Freedom we cry for. But strangely enough, we are not aware of the fact that we already have within us immense freedom. Look! Without any difficulty we can forget God. We can ignore Him and we can even deny Him. But God's Compassion says, "My children, no matter what you do or say, My Heart shall never abandon you. I want you. I need you."

The mother holds the hand of the child. But it is the child who has to walk, and he does so. Neither the one who is dragged nor the one who drags can be happy. Likewise God says, "My divine children, in your inner life, I give you inspiration. It is you who have to aspire with the purest heart to reach the Golden Beyond."

Sri Chinmoy

Concentration, meditation and contemplation

Concentration means total identification. You focus all your attention on something and identify yourself with the object or the subject. Then you receive and grow into its essence, its divine essence.

When you concentrate, you have to choose something that gives you immediate joy. If you have a Master, your Master's picture will give you immediate joy. If you don't have a Master, select something that is very beautiful, divine and pure. A flower has all of these qualities. You can concentrate on a flower or anything else that gives you joy. Look at the flower and, while looking at the flower, feel that you have entered into the flower and become the flower. Then, in a few minutes, try to feel that you have become one with the consciousness of the flower. There will be no thoughts, good or bad, remaining in the mind. When you become one with the flower, the fragrance of the flower and the divine qualities of the flower will enter into you.

Meditation

In the beginning you need a completely quiet place in which to concentrate. But if you are really advanced, at that time it does not matter. When I meditate and sing during a public function my concentration is very powerful. At that time it does not bother me when people are talking. But the talking may make other people unable to concentrate on my song. If I am concentrating here and somebody next to me is talking, I am totally unaware of him. I am in another world. But if someone starts making a noise, I will tell him to be quiet. It is not for my sake. Only I want to offer something, and if there is noise, then you will not be able to receive my offering.

After concentration comes meditation. In meditation, we enter into something vast. It may be Peace, Light or Bliss. When we get immense Peace, Light or Bliss in boundless measure, then we are meditating. When we meditate, we have to make our mind calm and quiet. This is absolutely necessary. If the mind is thinking of many things, then meditation can never happen.

Next we have to invoke the Presence of God. While invoking the Presence of God, we have to feel His constant inner guidance. Then, Peace, Light, Bliss and Power will descend. We can also get inner guidance from a spiritual Master. A Master can bring the soul of the seeker to the fore. The moment the soul comes forward, the heart immediately gets abundant joy and power. The power and joy of the heart then enter into the mind and the vital.

In terms of aspiration, the distances between concentration and meditation and meditation and contemplation are not the same. Between meditation and contemplation there is a very big gap. Many people do concentration when they have a great vital desire. If they want to become first in school or if they want to become a great football player, they will use tremendous vital power. When people are throwing the shot-put or doing the pole vault, tremendous willpower or concentration is needed. That is concentration from the vital. The power of concentration we automatically develop when we enter into sports. Athletes may not call it concentration. They only say, "My object is to throw the shotput farther than anybody." But that very idea or goal is concentration. But when it comes to meditation – making the mind calm, quiet, sublime and absolutely peaceful – that is too much for them. They will say that meditation has nothing to do with them. Again, many, many people on earth meditate or pray. Prayer and meditation are very similar. The only difference between prayer and meditation is that prayer goes up and meditation brings down. Both prayer and meditation are linked by a common goal. Prayer and meditation are like a see-saw. You are on one side and the Supreme is on the other side. You are going up and bringing down, but the Supreme remains on the other side.

Contemplation is a different process. During meditation and concentration, there is somebody with whom you are trying to be one. But in contemplation there is an interchange. You are playing two roles. At one moment you are what the Supreme is, on His side of the see-saw; you are on the same level with the Absolute. The next moment you are on the other side of the see-saw; He is acting as your Lord Supreme and you are acting as His supreme lover. Usually, the human mind is such that it says: "I have been worshipping Him all the time, so how can I be on the same level with Him?" But in contemplation this question does not arise. That is how contemplation is different from meditation and concentration.

Meditation and Self-discovery

The highest illumination is Self-discovery. This Self-discovery comes when we feel the need of the highest, deepest and all-transforming Reality in us. The all-transforming Reality is God the Wisdom, God the Compassion, God the Concern. If we go deep, deeper, deepest, to the inmost recesses of our heart we see God the eternal Concern, and in His Concern we see God the infinite Compassion. God's Compassion and God's Concern can never be separated.

What is the connecting link between our existence and God's Existence? The connecting link is our meditation. When we meditate on God we have to feel that this is the only language that we can use in order to speak to God. Then we see to our surprise that God also has the same language. He does not have a different language from ours. He also uses the same language, which is meditation. When we meditate we speak to Him. When He meditates, which He always does, He speaks to us. Meditation is the common language of man and God.

Our illumination starts the day we feel the necessity of constant meditation. Meditation has to be practised not only daily and regularly, but constantly. Inner meditation can take place at every moment. What is this inner meditation? It is the inner sacrifice. When we meditate inwardly, we are trying to sacrifice something. What is that something? It is the imperfection in us, which comes from ignorance. When we are ready to sacrifice our imperfection and ignorance, we feel that our vessel is totally empty. Now it has to be filled again. Ignorance is replaced with knowledge, and imperfection with perfection. By whom? By God.

Here we are all seekers, seekers of the infinite Truth. Here and now let us try to enter into the life of Reality, with our proper understanding of Truth. The Truth tells us: "Start where you are. If you have desire, start with your desire. If you have aspiration, start with your aspiration. But start! Do not wait. The Hour has struck; now it is up to you either to walk, march, run or fly." God is ready. Now we also have to be ready.

Everything is reciprocal. God gives us, in

infinite measure, what we give Him in infinitesimal measure. If we give Him an iota of love, He gives us in infinite measure His infinite Love. Again, when we go deep within we see that God is far above this reciprocal attitude. He does everything unconditionally in us and for us. He knows we are helpless, if not hopeless. He knows that He is the Doer, He is the Action and He is the Fruit thereof. He is the Player, He is the Game, He is the Result. But if we can consciously become one with His universal Will, then we will become a conscious instrument of His. Now we are His possession, but if we can become one with Him we will also grow into the Possessor Himself. This is what we mean by the highest illumination: when Possessor and possession become totally and inseparably one.

Sri Chinmoy

Prayer and meditation

A seeker who wants Peace, Bliss and divine Power in infinite measure will feel that prayer is not as important as meditation. When we pray, we try to elevate our entire consciousness. When we pray, we aspire towards the Highest and our whole existence goes upward like a flame. Prayer can come from the heart, but there is always a tendency in prayer to desire something. Since we are following a path of spirituality, naturally we will use our prayer to ask for something good, divine and fulfilling. But when we pray we automatically act as if we are beggars who are crying to God to grant us a boon.

When a beggar comes and knocks at the door, he does not care whether the owner is a rich man or a poor man; he just knocks and knocks in order to get something. This is the way we pray to God, asking for this and that, looking up at Him and crying to Him. We feel God is high above while we are down below. We see a yawning gulf between His existence and ours. We ask

Meditation

for things like a beggar asking a king for a coin. We do not know when or to what extent God is going to fulfil our desires. We just ask and then wait for one drop, two drops or three drops of Compassion, Light or Peace to descend upon us.

When we pray, there is an inherent subtle tendency on our part to push or pull from within. But when we meditate, we just try to throw ourselves into the Sea of Reality and grow into the Reality itself. Usually when we pray, Infinity, Eternity and Immortality do not immediately enter into our mind. Even though our prayer may be intense, it is only a tiny raft on which we are trying to cross the sea of ignorance. But when we meditate we become an ocean liner. At that time we can not only cross the sea with utmost safety and certainty, but also we can carry many along with us.

In prayer, unfortunately, our whole attention is on attaining one particular object. When we feel that the thing we have been crying for is achieved, our prayer often ends. We take a rest for a few months or a few years. Then when subtle desire prompts us, we begin to pray again.

When we meditate, it is nothing like that. In meditation we dive into the vast sea of Consciousness. We do not have to ask God for Peace or Light because we are swimming in the sea of divine qualities. At that time God gives us more than we can ever imagine. The deeper we go in meditation, the more we expand our own consciousness, the more abundantly the qualities of Light, Peace and Bliss grow inside us. Meditation itself is the fertile soil where the bumper crop of Light, Peace, Bliss and Power can grow.

In meditation there is a flame of constant aspiration. Our journey is eternal; our progress and our realisation are also constant and unending because we are dealing with Infinity, Eternity and Immortality.

In prayer we think of our own need and try to fulfil ourselves with God's help. In meditation, we throw ourselves into God's Consciousness and allow God to fulfil Himself in and through us. When we pray we act like beggars, but when we meditate we become princes. We see and feel that the whole universe is at our disposal. Heaven and earth do not belong to someone else. They are our own Reality which we cannot fully experience right now because we have lost it. But we are trying to regain it through our soulful meditation.

The way to get the utmost from meditation is to meditate according to the soul's necessities and demands. We must not feel that just because we are sitting quietly for five or ten minutes our meditation is going well. Meditation is not that easy. It requires conscious effort. The mind has to be made calm and quiet; at the same time, it has to be dynamic and vigilant like a fortress and not allow any enemies to enter. The heart must be like a pure and blossoming flower, opening fully to the light of the soul. The soul must come to the fore and spread its inner light all around. This is real, integral meditation.

In the highest spiritual life there is no comparison between meditation and prayer. Meditation is infinitely deeper and wider than prayer. In the West prayer is used by seekers with considerable efficacy. But a real seeker who wants to go to the ultimate Goal must feel that prayer is the lowest rung and meditation is the highest rung in the ladder of spiritual evolution to realisation. When we pray to God we ask God to fulfil us, to give us Peace, Love or Joy. When we meditate we expand, spreading our wings like a bird, trying to enter consciously into Infinity, Eternity and Immortality, welcoming them into our aspiring consciousness. We see, feel and grow into the entire universe of Light-Delight.

In prayer we have nothing and God has everything. That is why we say, "God, give me this." When we meditate we know that whatever God has, either we also have it or we will someday have it. We feel that whatever God is, we also are, but we have not brought it forward.

By praying wholeheartedly, we arrive at a certain consciousness where we get Peace, Light and Bliss, but this consciousness will not always be a certainty, nor will we receive it in infinite measure. Prayer immediately separates us from the Source, whereas meditation takes us to the Source or brings the Source to us. When we meditate we feel that we are growing into the highest divine Reality. A real seeker can do both. He can start with prayer and end with meditation. Prayer is like a hand grenade but meditation is like an atom bomb. Certainly in the beginning if he wants to pray, he should pray. But ultimately he will come to realise that he must pay more attention to meditation. Those who have started following my path sincerely and devotedly should give more importance to concentration, meditation and contemplation.

Love, devotion and surrender

Love, devotion and surrender. Love, devotion and surrender is our path. Love, devotion and surrender is our Goal.

Love. Love is the only wealth that man absolutely needs. Love is the only wealth that God precisely is.

Animal love can be conquered and purified. Human love can be perfected and transcended. Divine Love can be achieved and manifested.

To love God is to be a normal human being. To love God is to be a practical human being. To love God is to be a successful human being. To love God is to be a fulfilling and fulfilled human being.

Without love man is insecure. Without love man is uncertain. Without love man is incapable. Human insecurity is a chronic disease. Human uncertainty is an almost incurable disease. Human incapacity is a fatal disease.

God uses His Compassion-Power to transform our insecurity into His divine Security. God uses His Wisdom-Power to transform our uncertainty into His divine Certainty. God uses His Concern-Power to transform our human incapacity into His divine Capacity.

He who loves never grows old. God is a perfect example.

He who loves never becomes poor. God is a shining example.

He who loves never becomes unhappy. God is a blissful example.

Devotion. Devotion is our inner sweetness. Devotion is our divine intensity. Devotion is our supreme dynamism. God loves our snow-white sweetness. God appreciates our divine intensity. God admires our supreme dynamism.

A heart of devotion is purer than the purest flame. A heart of devotion is faster than the fastest deer. A heart of devotion is wiser than the wisest sage.

Purity's soulful permanence lives in devotion. Speed's truthful assurance lives in devotion. Wisdom's fruitful illumination lives in devotion.

Surrender. Surrender is our ever-increasing consciousness. Surrender is our ever-illumining vastness. Surrender is our ever-fulfilling oneness.

Consciousness is another name for the golden link between Heaven's descent and earth's ascent. Vastness is another name for God's Heart, which can be used by humanity. Oneness is another name for the evolving God in aspiring man.

Love, devotion and surrender: this is our path. All paths ultimately lead to the same destination, but we feel that the path of love, devotion and surrender is the safest and the quickest. This is our personal feeling. If others find it difficult to see eye to eye with us, they have every right to follow a different path. We will never say that ours is the only path and that only we will be able to offer salvation and illumination. No. Our path is for those who feel that the heart can lead them faster to their destination than the mind. Our path is for those who feel that the light of the soul has to come to the fore through the heart and that from the heart the light will be received by the mind, the vital and the physical.

Meditation

In our path love is the first rung of the ladder, devotion is the second rung and surrender is the third and ultimate rung. We love God because we feel that, of all His divine qualities, it is His Love that pleases us most. We love God, not because He is great, nor because He is Omniscient and Omnipotent and Omnipresent, not because He is everything; but rather we love God precisely because He is all Love, and Love is the mightiest power. Now when we love someone, we devote our existence to that person. Since it is God whom we love, it is to God that we offer our devotion. And it is to God's Will that we offer our human will. The surrender that we make to God is the conscious surrender of our soul to the Ultimate, the Absolute. This is not the surrender of a slave to his master but the surrender of our ignorant, unwilling, imperfect nature to our own illumining, liberated and perfected higher Being.

In our path we do not proselytise; we do not try to convert others. In our path we try to offer to others the Light that the Supreme has entrusted us with out of His infinite Bounty.

There are some who may say, "If you have Peace, Light and Bliss, why do you have to go all over the world to show it? Why do you have to go out and open Centres everywhere? If you own a pond, then anyone who is thirsty will come there to drink. The pond never goes to quench anyone's thirst. It remains where it is." But I wish to say that our path is the path of love, and that this is the kind of love that we see in a mother. When the child is hungry no matter if he is in the living room, the bedroom or the kitchen – no matter where he is – the mother comes running to offer food to him. Similarly, we feel that there are many sincere seekers who are hungry for Peace, Light and Bliss, and if we have received a little from the Almighty Supreme, we try to offer it to them. Like a shopkeeper, we offer certain things in our store, and those who like them may have them. Naturally, those who do not like what we have to offer have every right to go somewhere else. We will never say that our store is the only one.

Everybody has the right to inspire others. When we hold meditations we try to inspire people. We never expect to convert people to our path. That is far beyond our imagination. We try to offer inspiration through our talks and answers to questions. When we have played the role of giving inspiration, we feel that we have offered a considerable service. For it is from inspiration that all of us get aspiration, and it is from aspiration that we get realisation. No matter which path or which spiritual Master you follow, you are bound to get some inspiration. When you go deep within, on the strength of your inspiration you will see that your aspiration looms large. And when your aspiration-flame climbs high, higher, highest, you will realise your true Self.

III

POEMS ON MEDITATION

Meditation

MEDITATE, MEDITATE, MEDITATE!

Meditate, meditate, meditate!
Pay more attention to your meditation.
Spend more time in meditation.
Meditate soulfully, prayerfully and devotedly.

JUST A QUICK REMINDER

Just a quick reminder to meditate.
Meditate soulfully;
You will conquer ignorance-night
Easily.

Just a quick reminder to meditate.
Meditate unconditionally;
You will gain the Lord Supreme
Everlastingly.

THE MOST FRUITFUL TREASURES

Meditate, meditate, meditate!
You are bound to get
The most fruitful treasures,
But only if you can dare to ignore
The very idea of any reward.

THE SUPREME MEDITATES

Why does the Supreme want to meditate?
The Supreme wants to meditate
Because in His entire universe
He loves to enjoy only one thing,
And that is meditation.
Therefore, He sleeplessly meditates.
In His transcendental Life
And in His universal Life
The Supreme meditates.

Meditation

DON'T GIVE UP!

Pray and meditate;
Meditate and pray.
Don't give up!
If you give up,
Then you will be
As bad as the worst.

Pray and meditate;
Meditate and pray.
Reach the Goal.
No matter when you reach the Goal,
You will be
As good as the best.

MEDITATION

Meditation upon the unknown Thought
He thought was real meditation.
No, meditation is not and cannot be
On any thought.
Meditation is a conscious withdrawal
From the thought-world.
Meditation is the place
Where Reality, Divinity and Immortality
Can each claim their own
Perennial existence-light.

O SWEET MEDITATION!

O sweet meditation-flames,
You have brought me the message
   Of eternal silence.
You have given me courage indomitable.
You have given me patience interminable.
You have taught me how to be rich
   In mercy.
You have taught me how to drink
   Deep ecstasy.

Meditation

If you can offer gratitude to God
Before your meditation,
During your meditation
And after your meditation,
Then you will feel your progress-light
Clearing your mind-clouds.

Meditate, meditate, meditate
Soulfully, sleeplessly and self-givingly,
For meditation is nothing other than
Our supreme ignorance-shattering vision.

Meditate, meditate, meditate
Only on gratitude.
There shall come a time
When you are bound to feel and become
God's own Infinitude.

Sri Chinmoy

Meditation is
The expansion of consciousness.
When you are meditating,
If you feel and know
That along with you
Someone else will benefit
From your meditation,
Then this is absolutely perfect meditation.

Appendix

Bibliography

— Sri Chinmoy, *Meditation: God's Duty and man's beauty*, Agni Press, 1974. [MGD]

p11 Question: What is the aim of meditation?
p12 Question: What do we learn from meditation?
p15 Question: What is the highest meditation?
p16 Question: What is Light?
p18 Question: When you have a personal problem which you wish to solve through your meditation...
p20 Question: If we, your disciples, have questions about a course of action...
p157 What is meditation?

— Sri Chinmoy, *Earth's cry meets Heaven's Smile, part 2*, Aum Press, Puerto Rico, 1974. [ECH-2]

p 21 Question: How can I purify my mind so that I can have a good meditation?

— Sri Chinmoy, *Meditation: God's Blessing-Assurance*, Agni Press, 1974. [MGB]

p 23 Question: Is there anything specific I can do to have a good meditation every day?
p 26 Question: I'm not as receptive as I would like to be. Why is this?
p 29 Question: How can I increase my receptivity?
p 30 Question: How can you stop yourself from worrying

about whether you are having a good meditation or not?
p32 Question: How can I meditate with more intensity?
p33 Question: Are there any exercises your disciples can practise to develop their will-power?
p36 Question: How can we meditate on the soul?
p37 Question: The spiritual life and meditation should be the simplest of things; yet I always seem to complicate it. How can I keep my meditation simple?
p39 Question: How should we concentrate on your Transcendental Picture?
p199 Meditation and Self-Discovery

— Sri Chinmoy, *Spiritual power, occult power and will power*, Agni Press, 1976. [SPO]

p41 Question: How do you meditate?

— Sri Chinmoy, *My heart-door I have kept wide open*, Agni Press, 2011. [HDW]

p43 Question: Guru, when I am back at home working, I try to imagine you as often as possible in person...

— Sri Chinmoy, *The jewel of humility*, Agni Press, 1979. [JH]

p45 Question: Occasionally I see a little flash of light, a tiny light that goes in your eye and travels all around.

– Sri Chinmoy, *The hour of meditation*, Agni Press, 1977. [HM]

p47 Question: How can we meditate well?

p47 Question: Guru, how can we go deeper and deeper within so we can go beyond the surface mind?

p50 Question: I am strongly tuned to the mental plane. What can I do to enter into my inner being and feel my inner self more in my daily meditations?

p52 Question: What do you do when you are not one hundred per cent alert during meditation?

p53 Question: Is there any way to evaluate the result of our meditation?

– Sri Chinmoy, *Meditation: man's choice and God's Voice, part 1*, Agni Press, 1974. [MCV-1]

p55 Question: How can I see divine Light?

p60 Question: Why can't we get rid of all our undivine and negative forces permanently?

p60 Question: Can one overcome one's fears through meditation?

p64 Question: I am constantly bothered by thoughts during my meditation...

p65 Question: When I meditate, I sometimes feel a kind of pressure pushing in my mind.

— Sri Chinmoy, *Meditation: man's choice and God's Voice, part 2*, Agni Press, 1974. [MCV-2]

p66 Question: How can we discipline the mind?

p67 Question: Sometimes during my meditation I feel I am attacked by very undivine thoughts. How can I fight against them?

p69 Question: Always when I try to go beyond the mind, it says, "No, carry me with you. I want to go there, too."

p70 Question: Why do you want us to meditate in the heart? I find it easier to meditate in the mind.

p75 Question: Sometimes during my meditation I find that my mind seems to be dwelling on worldly or unspiritual thoughts.

p76 Question: What kind of attitude should you have when you meditate on the heart?

p77 Question: What is the best way to meditate during action?

— Sri Chinmoy, *Meditation: God speaks and I listen, part 1*, Vishma Press, 1974. [MGS-1]

p79 Question: How do you go about emptying your mind in order to be able to meditate?

p79 Question: How do you do it?

— Sri Chinmoy, *Meditation: God speaks and I listen, part 2*, Sri Chinmoy Lighthouse, 1974. [MGS-2]

p80 Question: How should we meditate on the picture of a spiritual Master?

p81 Question: When I meditate, I imagine you giving me a blessing at that moment. Is this blessing real?

p82 Question: Was the Peace and inner Bliss that I felt here last Wednesday night a sign that I had been initiated?

— Sri Chinmoy, *Meditation: humanity's race and Divinity's Grace, part 1*, Agni Press, 1974. [MRG-1]

p83 Question: How do you learn to concentrate?

p86 Question: The moment I sit down to meditate, all kinds of silly or ugly thoughts come into my mind.

p87 Question: It is difficult for me to concentrate on my heart for longer than just a few minutes.

p89 Question: When we want to concentrate or meditate on a special thought or problem, how should we do it?

p91 Question: In our meditation, can we consciously invoke our soul? And if so, how?

p93 Question: Would you speak a little about proper breathing in meditation?

– Sri Chinmoy, *Meditation: humanity's race and Divinity's Grace, part 2*, Agni Press, 1974. [MRG-2]

p97 Question: How can we know whether we are meditating well or not?

p188 Meditation: an introduction

– Sri Chinmoy, *The meditation-world*, Agni Press, 1977. [MW]

p99 Question: Is there anything I can do to always have a good meditation?

– Sri Chinmoy, *The mind and the heart in meditation*, Agni Press, 1977. [MHM]

p100 Question: When I meditate with my heart on your picture I've been getting a headache.

p101 Question: How can one discipline the mind during meditation?

p103 Question: After I have a good meditation I lose it. What can I do to maintain my meditation?

p104 Question: What should we imagine if we are very tired during our morning meditation?

p194 Concentration, meditation and contemplation

— Sri Chinmoy, *Experiences of the higher worlds*, Agni Press, 1977. [EHW]

p104 Question: How can one still one's mind in meditation?
p106 Question: How can I recognise a spiritual experience as such?
p108 Question: I would like to know the best and the most effective way to raise one's consciousness and to maintain that level.

— Sri Chinmoy, *Kundalini: the Mother-Power,* Aum Press, 1973. [KMP]

p109 Question: Does sexual indulgence prevent one from acquiring occult power through Kundalini Yoga?
p110 Question: Is there a particular centre I can meditate on in order to control my thoughts?
p111 Question: What is the relationship between the third eye and the heart centre?
p115 Question: If you feel warmth in the region of the heart, is this a sign of the heart centre opening up?

— Sri Chinmoy, *Prayer-world, mantra-world and japa-world*, Agni Press, 1974. [PWM]

p115 Question: Do you recommend the use of any special mantra?
p116 Question: What is the significance of the Gayatri mantra?

p117 Question: Can you please tell us about a few other mantras?
p120 Question: What happens when we chant AUM?
p121 Question: How are we actually supposed to chant AUM?
p202 Prayer and meditation

– Sri Chinmoy, *Promised Light from the Beyond*, AUM Publications, New York, 1973. [PLB]

p123 Question: Before beginning meditation and concentration, I was wondering if there should be a specific manner of breathing.
p126 Question: How can I purify my mind so that I can have a good meditation?
p128 Question: How is it possible to keep one's mind from having any thoughts?

– Sri Chinmoy, *The summits of God-Life: Samadhi and Siddhi*, Agni Press, 1974. [SGL]

p130 Question: How can one recognise a God-realised spiritual Master?
p132 Question: Is there a specific way to accelerate realisation?
p134 Question: When I think of all the failings and undivine qualities in myself and my fellow disciples, illumination seems a million miles away.

— Sri Chinmoy, *Purity-river wins*, Agni Press, 1974. [PRW]

p135 Question: What can we do during our meditation to transform or to help purify the mind, vital and body?

p136 Question: What is the most effective way I can attain purity?

— Sri Chinmoy, *Sri Chinmoy speaks, part 1*, Agni Press, 1976. [SCS-1]

p138 Question: How can I maintain my inner strength during my meditation?

— Sri Chinmoy, *Sri Chinmoy speaks, part 7*, Agni Press, 1976. [SCS-7]

p140 Question: What is the best way to deal with dry periods in one's sadhana?

— Sri Chinmoy, *My meditation-service at the United Nations for twenty-five years*, Agni Press, 1995. [MUN]

p142 Question: Sometimes when I meditate, I feel that I am about to go through some experience, but nothing happens. What is the cause of that?

p145 Question: How can our imagination be used to help raise our consciousness or improve our meditation?

– Sri Chinmoy, *Flame-Waves, part 4*, Agni Press, 1975. [FW-4]

p145 Question: How can I have deeper meditation?

– Sri Chinmoy, *God-Journey's Perfection-Return*, Agni Press, 1975. [GJ]

p149 Question: After we stop meditating, how can we maintain the level of consciousness we reached during our meditation?

– Sri Chinmoy, *Dependence and assurance*, Agni Press, 1975. [DA]

p163 Individual meditation

– Sri Chinmoy, *Eastern light for the Western mind*, Agni Press, 1973. [EL]

p177 The supreme secret of meditation

– Sri Chinmoy, *The oneness of the Eastern heart and the Western mind, part 3*, Agni Press, 2004. [OEH-3]

p182 Meditation
p208 Love, devotion and surrender

– Sri Chinmoy, *A child's heart and a child's dreams*, Aum Publications, 1986. [CHD]

p186 Meditation

– Sri Chinmoy, *Ten Thousand Flower-Flames, part 57*, Agni Press, 1983. [FF-57]

p 217 MEDITATE, MEDITATE, MEDITATE!

– Sri Chinmoy, *Ten Thousand Flower-Flames, part 5*, Agni Press, 1979. [FF-5]

p 217 JUST A QUICK REMINDER

– Sri Chinmoy, *Ten Thousand Flower-Flames, part 47*, Agni Press, 1982. [FF-47]

p 218 THE MOST FRUITFUL TREASURES

– Sri Chinmoy, *Ten Thousand Flower-Flames, part 49*, Agni Press, 1982. [FF-49]

p 219 THE SUPREME MEDITATES

– Sri Chinmoy, *The Wings of Light, part 2*, Aum Press, Puerto Rico, 1974. [WL-2]

p219 DON'T GIVE UP!

– Sri Chinmoy, *Transcendence-Perfection,* Agni Press, 1975. [TP]
p220 MEDITATION

– Sri Chinmoy, *A Soulful Cry Versus a Fruitful Smile,* Agni Press, 1977. [SC]
p220 O SWEET MEDITATION!

– Sri Chinmoy, *Twenty-Seven Thousand Aspiration-Plants, part 227,* Agni Press, 1996. [AP-227]
p221

– Sri Chinmoy, *Twenty-Seven Thousand Aspiration-Plants, part 239,* Agni Press, 1997. [AP-239]
p221, p, 221

– Sri Chinmoy, *Twenty-Seven Thousand Aspiration-Plants, part 94,* Agni Press, 1984. [AP-94]
p222

The heart-traveller

1. Aspiration-Flames — Aspiration and God's Hour
2. A Sri Chinmoy primer
3. Everest-Aspiration
4. New Year's Messages from Sri Chinmoy (1966-2007)
5. Flower-Flames
6. Songs of the Soul
7. Eternity's Breath
8. Meditation

www.ingramcontent.com/pod-product-compliance
Lightning Source LLC
Chambersburg PA
CBHW030257100526
44590CB00012B/425